one child, many worlds

EARLY LEARNING IN MULTICULTURAL COMMUNITIES

Eve Gregory, editor

language and literacy series

Teachers College
Columbia University
New York and London

Published in the United States of America by Teachers College Press
1234 Amsterdam Avenue, New York, NY 10027

Published in Great Britain by David Fulton Publishers 1997

Cataloging-in-Publication Data available through the Library of Congress

ISBN: 0-8077-3715-1

Manufactured in Great Britain

01 00 99 98 97   5 4 3 2 1

Contents

12/28/98-20.55-134

Preface

We are fortunate to be able to draw upon many detailed examples of young monolingual children as they set about learning at home. We are often struck by the skills these children display as they participate in story-reading, writing or socio-dramatic play with their parents. Generally, these activities are recognisable in the experience of our own families; we repeat them with our younger siblings, our children or grandchildren. Yet we have few similar examples of the learning taking place in the lives of young children whose home language and literacy practices might be very different from those represented in school. In this collection of case studies, readers are invited into the worlds of eleven such children. Ten of the children are emergent bilinguals; the eleventh is a monolingual child who is shortly to begin a Jewish school in London. Each study reveals the wealth of knowledge of the children, as well as the skills and patience of their 'teachers' at home and in the community. The home 'teachers' are siblings, grandparents, parents, community class teachers, friends, films and videos. Learning about cultural and linguistic differences is not an easy task for it involves admitting what one does not know. I hope that this book will inspire early years educators everywhere to take the courage to go into the communities to find out. Only in this way can we show all our families the respect they deserve.

Eve Gregory, Querétaro, México.
January, 1997

The contributors

Inge Cramer has worked in a variety of schools in Suffolk and Bradford, both as a class teacher and as a language support teacher. She was joint co-ordinator for the National Oracy Project in Bradford before becoming a primary advisory teacher on language for the English National Curriculum.[1] She is now a senior lecturer in the Department of Teaching Studies at Bradford and Ilkley Community College. Her current research focuses on oral storymaking in a multilingual school.

Rose Drury is co-ordinator of a primary Section 11 team in Watford. (Section 11 teachers are funded partly by the British Government and partly by the local education authority to teach children with English as their second language.) In addition, she is co-ordinating a pre-school community-based project in Hertfordshire. She has extensive experience of teaching bilingual children in the early years and is a nursery education OfSTED (Office for Standards in Education) inspector. She is currently carrying out research into the pre-school years for an M Phil at Goldsmiths' College, University of London.

Eve Gregory is Reader in Educational Studies at Goldsmiths' College, University of London, where she works with students on undergraduate, postgraduate and research degrees. She has directed projects supported by the Paul Hamlyn Foundation and the Economic and Social Research Council (ESRC) investigating children's out-of-school reading and the transfer of cognitive strategies between home and school. In 1997 she was awarded a Leverhulme Research Fellowship arising from this work. She is author of *Making Sense of a New World: Learning to read in a second language* (Paul Chapman, 1996). Both her research and her teaching call

1   National Curriculum studies are compulsory for all schools in England and Wales.

upon her former experience as an early years teacher in multilingual classrooms.

Joan Kale is a sociolinguist and teacher educator at Batchelor College in Australia's Northern Territory. Previously she taught at James Cook University in North Queensland and has published widely on language education in Aboriginal contexts. She presently is working facilitating and developing indigenous teacher education programmes in remote communities.

Charmian Kenner conducted doctoral research into multilingualism and early writing at Southampton University. She is now an associate lecturer in education for the Open University and an associate research fellow at the Centre for Applied Linguistic Research, Thames Valley University. She has contributed to several publications for teachers of bilingual children and also to in-service training courses. Her future research plans include a longitudinal study of children learning to write in more than one language.

Susi Long received her doctorate from Ohio State University. She works as a consultant to international schools and local school districts, and as an adjunct professor for the University of South Carolina. Her research interests include cross-cultural adjustment, second-language acquisition and literacy development.

Allan Luke is Professor of Education at the University of Queensland, Brisbane, Australia, where he teaches literacy education and educational sociology. His books on literacy include *Literacy, Textbooks and Ideology* (Falmer, 1988), *The Social Construction of Literacy in the Primary Classroom* (Macmillan, 1994) and *Constructing Critical Literacies*, edited with Peter Freebody and Sandy Muspratt (Hampton/Allen & Unwin, 1997). He is currently working on issues of Asian identity in families, schooling and public discourse.

Pamela Oberhuemer is a researcher at the State Institute of Early Childhood Education and Research (IFP) in Munich. Her research interests include learning and teaching in multicultural contexts and cross-national perspectives on early years education. With Michaela Ulich, she has edited a series of books and audio-visual materials for teachers, focusing on ethnic stories and childlore as a starting point for inter-cultural dialogue. Together they have recently completed a survey of staff training for work in early years settings in the 15 European Union countries. Pamela is an editorial board member of the *International Journal of Early Years Education.*

Nasiima Rashid has been involved in the literacy development of bilingual children both as a practising teacher and as a research officer on projects funded by Goldsmiths' College, the Paul Hamlyn Foundation and the ESRC. She undertook her own research in the field of bilingualism and literacy when completing an MA at the Institute of Education, University of London. She applies her findings from this research in her work as classroom teacher at an Inner-London Primary school.

Leena Robertson was born and grew up in Finland and, as a mother of two bilingual children, feels that 'Finnishness' is still an important part of her identity. All her training and professional work has taken place in Britain, in her second language. She completed an MA in Language and Literature in Education in 1995, and is now completing a doctoral thesis in bilingual children's early literacy development at Goldsmiths' College, University of London. She also works full-time as a mainstream class teacher, currently responsible for a reception/year one class.

Maureen Turner began teaching bilingual children in inner-city Birmingham in 1972, where she developed an interest in special needs, and was seconded to a certificate course at the West Midlands College. She also has successfully completed the bilingualism and special needs course at the Institute of Education, University of London. She is at present assistant team leader in the Bilingual Learners' Support Service in Southampton, and is a teacher and tutor on the Hampshire certificate course in teaching English in multilingual schools. Her current research interests include the assessment of bilingual pupils and parental involvement in reading.

Michaela Ulich is a researcher at the IFP in Munich. Her special fields of research, publication and in-service training have been intercultural education and learning, children's perspectives and early childhood education in European Union countries.

Dinah Volk is an Associate Professor and Co-ordinator of the Early Childhood Program at the College of Education, Cleveland State University. Her research, described in journals and edited volumes, focuses on the language and literacy development of young bilingual children and the support their families provide for their learning. Her on-going work with teachers on multicultural curriculum development is reflected in *Kaleidoscope: A multicultural approach for the primary school classroom*, a source book for teachers written with Y. De Gaetano and L.R. Williams. Before teaching at university, Dr Volk worked for many years with three and four year olds in day-care settings, and six and seven year olds in public and parent-co-operative schools.

Ann Williams worked as a teacher for many years before completing her doctoral research on the use of non-standard dialect in children's school writing. Since then she has carried out ESRC-funded research on new town dialects, the role of children in language change, and literacy in school and the community. She is currently co-director and research fellow on an ESRC-funded project, *The Role of Adolescents in Dialect Levelling,* in the Department of Linguistic Science at the University of Reading.

Acknowledgements

The authors wish to acknowledge their debt of gratitude to all the families and teachers involved in this work. Individual acknowledgements are included at the end of each chapter.

This book is dedicated to children everywhere who must begin school in a language which is not their own.

Chapter 1

Introduction

Eve Gregory

'We come to every situation with stories: patterns and sequences of events which are built into us. Our learning happens within the experience of what important others did.' (Bateson, 1979:13)

The eleven children whom we meet in this book bring very different stories and experiences to their first classrooms. They enter school or pre-school in five countries and between them speak, read or write twelve languages. Nelson, alone, will attend a bilingual Spanish/English kindergarten classroom. Elsey, a Torres Strait Creole speaker from Australia will begin an English-speaking Kindy; Zeynep is a Turkish speaker who will begin pre-school in German; and Kelli, an American child, must quickly master Icelandic in her new home. The other children all enter nursery or infant classes in Britain bringing with them a wealth of languages. Nazma and Imrul speak fluent Pahari (a Panjabi dialect); at three, Meera begins writing in Gujarati; Maruf speaks Sylheti, Zohra is a Panjabi speaker; and Rameen speaks, and is beginning to read, Urdu. In addition, Imrul and Maruf are both learning to read and write in the standard form of their language as well as practising the Qur'an in Arabic. All these children are emergent bilinguals who will need to use English in school. Nadia, our only monolingual child, introduces us to a world of different reading activities in her East London home.

The hubbub of the early years classroom makes it easy to forget the importance of shared rituals and experiences in enabling children to feel a sense of *belonging* to a group. The children in this book have in common home and community experiences which, generally, are not those legitimised by the school and which, in most cases, bear very little resemblance to the childhood memories of their teachers. Unlike many socially advantaged pupils, Elsey and the other children in the group will not enter school familiar with the language and behaviour rituals, or 'recipes' (Hymes, 1974), of the classroom. In most cases, their families will not share the practice of reading stories at home, nor can the children automatically use appropriate linguistic recipes: 'please', 'thank-you', 'it hurts' etc – all still need time and thought. Thus, they are not yet members of the language and culture represented and validated in their schools.

These eleven children, then, enter classrooms possessing a different kind of knowledge from that which will be expected in school. The crucial question asked by all the contributors to this book is: 'how can teachers find out about, and build upon, this knowledge in their classroom practice?' What follows are personal accounts by experienced classroom practitioners of their findings as they worked with an individual child, the child's family and the wider community. Although each case deserves careful study and discussion, the papers collectively offer a new framework of principles for those working in multicultural communities. Together, the authors in this book challenge some very basic assumptions existing in early childhood practice today.

Early childhood practice in multicultural communities: the challenge

Background

A fundamental principle of early childhood education in the western world has been the acknowledgement of children's *individuality*. In this respect, Piaget's theory of child development (1971), which stressed both the way in which children actively *construct* their own intelligence and meanings and the progressive development of logical structures (schemas) which describe the *stage* a child has reached, has been seminal. Piaget's dual focus on the individual construction of meaning and a common set of stages through which all children pass, has underpinned assumptions of the *universality* of learning and learning practices across cultures.

A second important principle informing early-childhood education has been that of the *interpersonal* nature of the learning process. Here, Vygotsky's (1962) representation of learning as that which takes place within the 'zone of proximal development' or ZPD (the gap between a child's present learning and what can be achieved with the assistance of an adult or more knowledgeable person), and Bruner's (1986) metaphor of 'scaffolding' (the support system offered by an older person to a young child), have been crucial. Within this framework, the role of the teacher is to provide support or assist each child individually across the zone.

Although both Vygotsky and Bruner's work may be interpreted on a socio-cultural plane with far more complex implications, it has been more manageable for classroom practitioners to concentrate on the one-to-one interaction between teacher and child. As a consequence, Bruner's notion of a 'joint culture creation' between pupil and teacher has often been seen as unproblematic as long as teachers have a firm grounding in general theories of child language and development.

The problem for us when dealing with our eleven children is that none of the afore-mentioned works gives particular consideration to pupils entering school with different languages and/or cultural practices from those of their teachers. Similarly, many language-acquisition studies, which have been influential in teacher training courses (Halliday, 1975, and Wells, 1987), present examples of western monolingual children who share the language and cultural practices of the researcher and their future teachers. Studies on early literacy teaching in western countries (Wells, 1987 and Waterland, 1988) have also mainly reflected the practices of researchers themselves, whereby the experience of written narrative and the importance of talking about stories as a precursor for reading have been viewed as vital first steps for early literacy success.

Studies into linguistic and, especially, cultural differences have not exerted much influence on the work of early childhood practitioners. This is partly due to a lack of information on the subject during initial training courses and partly, no doubt, due to the wish of most of their children's families quietly to adapt to the dominant language and practices of the school. In Britain, recognition of 'differences' has been further complicated by the influence of the work of Basil Bernstein (1971) and the uncomfortable association of difference with deficit. In an attempt to counteract any suggestion of this, early childhood educators have tended to avoid discussion on cultural differences between children. Yet this position holds obvious dangers, as highlighted by many of the contributors to this book. If western school-oriented learning practices, such as narrative experience and active engagement with play provision in the nursery are viewed as universal, and if the children in this book are judged by their performance in such practices, then all will be seen to be deficient. Yet each child displays impressive linguistic and cognitive skills which, in most cases, are well beyond the reach of their teachers. As the authors in this volume argue, we need a new framework of principles within which to record these skills and to guide early years work in multicultural communities.

A new framework for practice

Contributors to this book draw largely upon studies of early learning in a cross-cultural context. The work of Barbara Rogoff and her team (1993), who are documenting the very different learning practices negotiated by caregivers and toddlers in 'guided participation' across the world, has proved inspirational to a number of authors. Likewise, the work of Shirley Brice-Heath (1983) and Sarah Michaels (1986) in the *Ways with Words* and stories of children from different cultural backgrounds; and Luis Moll and his team (1992) who are investigating the 'funds of knowledge' held by Hispanic families in the United States, have provided examples of innovative practice. Studies by Street (1984) and Luke (1994), arguing for literacy to be viewed as a social and ideological construct, rather than a neutral skill, also underpin a number of contributions. Finally, the work of Alessandro Duranti and Eleanor Ochs (1996), revealing the syncretic nature of literacy practices of Samoan Americans, highlights the dynamic nature of culture in the hands of the young. All the authors in this volume argue against notions of universality or 'naturalness' of learning practices and propose that, as educators, we must take account of the multiple pathways of learning in children's worlds. This means recognising that there will be different mediators of language and literacy in children's lives who may well operate using materials, methods and rules of inter-action which are unknown to us.

What might this recognition look like in classroom practice? The following five principles and associated questions are developed by each contributor to the book.

Principle one: Find out about the funds of knowledge brought by children into nursery or school.

• General questions to ask:
   (a) What advantages might this knowledge have for the child?
   (b) Who and what are the mediators of this knowledge in the child's life outside school? (parents, siblings, grandparents, other relatives, friends, community class teachers, videos, films, etc.)
   (c) What approaches, materials and methods might they use?
   (d) How is a syncretism of language and learning practices taking place? In what ways?

• More specific questions on language:
   (a) Which languages can the child understand, speak, distinguish or reproduce?

(b) How far is the child able to transfer knowledge from one language to another?

(c) How far can the child switch languages/dialects?

(d) How far is the child aware of differences between languages? How far is the child able to explain words and concepts to assist others?

(e) Does a beginner to the new language show a wish to communicate non-verbally?

- More specific questions on children's outside school-literacy practices:
  (a) What effect might experience of the following have on a child's interpretation of reading and writing in school?
    - community language, Qur'anic or other religious classes?
    - television, films, videos, stories?
    - exposure to a written script in different languages?
    - reading non-fiction adult books with different caregivers?
    - home Bible-reading sessions?

Principle two: Devise classroom approaches which use children's home knowledge as their inspiration.

- Questions to ask:
  (a) How can the parameters of the classroom be widened?
  (b) How can children's home knowledge be used in the classroom and who might be able to assist in this?
  (c) How can children experiment and play with new rules (linguistic and cultural) they might find in the classroom?

Principle three: Establish in what ways children's out-of-school knowledge might differ from what counts as learning in school, as well as own knowledge.

- Questions to ask:
  (a) What are the rules of your classroom? What counts as learning (especially during language and literacy activities) in the classroom?
  (b) How implicit/explicit are these rules (especially politeness routines, participation rules, etc.)?
  (c) What counts as 'reading' (when and how to talk about a book etc.)?

Principle four: Find ways in which classroom rules can be made more explicit to children who are unfamiliar with them.

- Questions to ask:
  (a) Can role-play, stories and storying be used to this end?

Principle five: Consider in what ways continuities in home and school language and learning practices may be strengthened, and how discontinuities might be a springboard for learning

- Questions to ask:
  (a) How can children, teachers and families become more aware of new cultural practices through a comparison with those they already know?

Although many of our eleven children appear to begin school with all the odds against them, the authors look with optimism to each child's future success. We see numerous examples of gifted mediators of language and literacy and many of these are the teachers themselves. An important aim of all the authors was to trace their own learning process while the study was conducted. Most teachers will be able to translate this learning into their own work with a child like Elsey, Nazma, Nadia or even Kelli in their classrooms.

The importance of the teacher's own discoveries is perhaps best summed up by Robertson who concludes the volume. Robertson traces her own childhood education in Finland to her realisation with five-year-old Imrul that what counts as learning in school is culturally and historically based. She documents her surprise as she recognises that what counted as valid learning during her teacher training was very different from both her own childhood experiences and those of Imrul in his Qur'anic class. Like all the authors, she concludes that while it is impossible to pretend that the cultural rules of the school do not exist, it is nonetheless important to recognise that what takes place in school reflects only one set of rules which are both time and place specific: not *better* but simply *different* from rules elsewhere. Within this framework, her role as teacher will be to identify and build upon Imrul's home learning, while simultaneously explicitly introducing him to the vocabulary of formal education in the host country. Robertson's final statement that, after all, Karelia is not so far from Kashmir, reflects both the joy expressed by all the authors in learning about new practices and their humility in understanding their own.

References

Bateson, G. (1979) *Mind and Nature*. London: Wildwood House.

Bernstein, B. (1971) *Class, Codes and Control*. London: Routledge & Kegan Paul.

Bruner, J. (1986) *Actual Minds, Possible Worlds*. Cambridge, Mass: Harvard University Press.

Duranti, A. and Ochs, E. (1996) *Syncretic Literacy: Multiculturalism in Samoan American families*. National Center for Research on Cultural Diversity and Second Language Learning, University of California, Santa Cruz.

Halliday, M.A.K. (1975) *Learning How to Mean: Explorations in the development of language*. London: Edward Arnold.

Heath, S.B. (1983) *Ways with Words: Language, life and work in communities and classrooms*. Cambridge: Cambridge University Press.

Hymes, D. (1974) *Foundations in Sociolinguistics*. Philadelphia: University of Philadelphia Press.

Luke, A. (1994) *The Social Construction of Literacy in the Classroom*. Melbourne: Macmillan.

Michaels, S. (1986) 'Narrative Presentations: An oral preparation for literacy with 1st. graders' in Cook-Gumperz, J. (Ed.) *The Social Construction of Literacy*. Cambridge: Cambridge University Press.

Moll, L., Amanti, C., Neff, D. and Gonzalez, N. (1992) Funds of Knowledge for Teaching: Using a qualitative approach to connect homes and classrooms', *Theory into Practice*, Vol.XXXI, No.2, (132–41).

Piaget, J. (1971) *Science of Education and the Psychology of the Child*. London: Longman.

Rogoff, B., Mosier, C., Mistry, J. and Göncü, A. (1993) 'Toddlers' guided participation with their caregivers in cultural activity' in Forman, E., Minick, N. and Stone, C. (Eds) *Contexts for Learning*. New York: Oxford University Press.

Street, B. (1984) *Literacy in Theory and Practice*. Cambridge: Cambridge University Press.

Vygotsky, L. (1962) *Thought and Language*. Cambridge, Mass: MIT Press.

Waterland, L. (1988) *Read with Me: An apprenticeship approach to reading*. Bath: The Thimble Press.

Wells, C.G. (1987) *The Meaning Makers: children learning language and using language to learn*. Portsmouth, NH: Heinemann.

Part I

Setting the Scene: The Multiple Worlds of Children's Learning

In Part One, Luke and Kale introduce key questions which will recur in different ways throughout the book. Using the example of Elsey, a child who speaks mainly Torres Strait Creole (TSC) at home, they ask two major questions. 'How will we judge her first attempts at expressing herself in a new language in school? How will it be possible to interpret her language and literacy skills by her classroom performance?' Luke and Kale confront squarely the danger of stereotyping when a child does not share the learning practices expected by the school. The authors then carefully unpick Elsey's skills in her different languages and propose a framework for investigating early language socialisation in cross-cultural contexts. Crucial within this framework is the recognition that the differences brought by children to classrooms are too predictable to reflect simply individual differences; they are the products and constructions of social learnings from the cultures where the children live and interact. The authors then go on to show that different cultures make meaning in different ways, with different patterns of exchange and interaction, different text conventions and different beliefs about reading and writing. Children like Elsey learn to live in multiple worlds, to switch from one language or literacy practice to another, each with its corresponding set of rules. The nature of these different worlds and how children learn to live in them is taken up in each of the other ten studies which follow.

Chapter 2

Learning through difference: cultural practices in early childhood language socialisation

Allan Luke and Joan Kale

Introduction: literacy and difference

> Tell you 'baut the crocodile first.
> Well, this crocodile 'e small tha/watnau? the chicken smell.
> It's a raw one.
> It's not a cook one
> but they eat raw one.
> So... this first big crocodile where they wanna send them away
> well, 'e smell/ 'e's/ take the smell of it,
> so 'e went down an' jus' stop...
> *Elsey, Age 6*

It is Monday morning early in the school year, and a year one class is sitting around the rug area swapping stories. Above is the beginning of one six-year-old's contribution. Read it again and try to 'hear' her contribution. Pause for a moment and consider this before reading on: what judgments could we make about the child?

We might conclude that her choice of topics was not appropriate for classroom talk. That it was too imaginary or, for that matter, too realistic. Or that she does not speak English 'properly'. Or we might infer that she has not been read stories by her parents. However naive, erroneous or dangerous such stereotypes are, they operate in the classroom almost continually. They tend to guide our everyday decisions about children – decisions that have effects, even in future life. Such stereotypes can be based on what we might call 'deficit thinking', ways that seek out 'lack' in children's talk and behaviour. Instead, our aim here is to provide tools to recognise what the differences in this child's spoken language might tell us about her experiences, knowledge and her use of words.

In this chapter we introduce a vocabulary for discussing the development of language and literacy, and for understanding the relationship of the diverse knowledge and practices children bring from community cultures to the social and language environments of the school. Following this, we turn to a closer description of Elsey's language learning and use in her home and community. There we explore some of the ways she uses language with friends and family, and what she knows about literacy and print. We also look at how she combines the texts of her community traditions with those of popular culture to develop a distinctive identity and world view. Finally, we introduce some ways of teaching literacy in order to achieve equal access for all children towards powerful practices with text – whether social, academic or cultural – a goal which needs to be at the forefront of all early childhood education.

First, a brief aside on what are often presented as 'normal' or 'natural' patterns of child development. Much of the search to describe universal patterns or stages of child development was based on the work of early 20th-century European, British and American child psychologists, who focused their work on descriptions of middle-class monocultural and monolingual urban children, particularly males. As we will explain here, language socialisation is contingent on the social relations and cultural practices of the increasingly-diverse communities where children grow up. Understanding diversity or 'difference' is now the norm across the school systems of English-speaking countries.

When we speak of the 21st century as times of difference, we mean that our student populations are multicultural, with dynamic blendings of identities and of cultures. In everyday lives we mix the texts of popular culture with longstanding community and cultural practices and traditions. The results are new and unprecedented forms of expression: rap music and poetry; new methods of print and multimedia and on-line expression; new forms of workplace literacy; and new genres of writing in newspapers, fiction and magazines (Buckingham and Sefton-Green, 1995). People everywhere are inventing and reinventing their identities to fit new kinds of work, communities, and social practices. This is leading to changes in family configurations, gender roles, relations between children and adults and, indeed, relations between teachers and students.

Apprenticing at language in homes and communities

Children are learning language from infancy. Instances of daily social interaction – meals, bedtime, clearing up, play, television, arguments – are moments of language use and learning. In effect, children learn by apprenticing: by watching, learning, practising, mimicking, transforming and absorbing the ways with words used in the social sites by those around them. Everyday life is thus a complex fabric of speech events, where that apprenticeship takes place. But these events, instances where people use and learn language, are not altogether random or spontaneous or 'creative'. They are rule-governed and goal-seeking: that is, speech events often unconsciously follow unstated cultural rules and conventions that are rehearsed, constructed and, quite frequently, resisted and broken each day in communities. To make meaning, we adhere to (and regularly stretch and break) social conventions which dictate who can speak – when, how, about what – when to be silent, what is an appropriate comment, how to take turns in conversation, who has more power in talk, gesture and other aspects of communication. People thus are *semiotic* beings: they use and interpret signs and signals to make meaning and to achieve social purposes in the world.

Calling out for food or a toy, telling a tale, arguing with another child, bending the truth to avoid punishment – these are all cases where children are working with words. But, it is worth remembering, the word choices and sentence structures, the idioms and actual practices for doing these things are not universal and, by definition, they vary greatly across communities. This is not simply a matter of individual difference. That is too simple and convenient an answer when there are such visible patterns and continuities of practice shared by members of communities. Different cultures make meaning in different ways, with different patterns of exchange and interaction, text conventions and beliefs about reading and writing.

To see patterns at work, consider common speech events such as telephone conversations, gossip, or a university seminar. Specific topics ('what kind of car you drive'), utterances ('Did you see what he was doing last night?') or gestures (an embrace) – perhaps appropriate for a private conversation – might be inappropriate in a public seminar situation. In a broad range of such speech events, speakers use language to establish and negotiate their social identities, and they are defined and constituted by the language and discourse used (Kress, 1989). From early childhood to adulthood, we use language to explain and express ourselves, to position and control others. At the same time our identities and positions are defined, constructed and 'framed' by language in use. As we will see later, Elsey draws from diverse cultural sources to construct an identity for herself.

For another example of learned rules and conventions at work, consider those in play when you are served at a take-away food outlet and prepare to give your order ('Good afternoon, welcome to.... May I take your order please?... Would you like a drink with that?'). In this typical encounter, the institutional site defines and constrains the participants' aims and possibilities for meaning. The participants are playing to certain segments of the community a well-known and frequently-rehearsed script. Particular service roles frame what can be said and done by the service worker, the consumer, the manager, and so forth. Further, a disruption of the rules may cause misunderstanding and miscommunication, and perhaps a botched order. Of course, speakers quite often bend, break and strain against rules of particular sites, but they generally do so for particular purposes and effects (for example, to shock, to upset, to amuse, to change the power relations).

In summary, children grow in, and through, a range of speech events in homes and communities, experimenting with, and developing ways of, doing things with words. Children learn and experiment with when they can speak, when it might be appropriate to 'talk back' to an adult or peer, where they can discuss topics which might be considered 'personal', how to express emotions, what kind of things can be said, for instance, at mealtime or bedtime, etc. This is not a matter of value-free, neutral skill acquisition. As part of this socialisation, they are engaging with a complex fabric of cultural values and ideologies regarding, among other things, gender, race, age and authority relations and power. In this sense, they are not apprenticing at language *per se* – they are apprenticing at membership of various cultures and communities.

Thus, virtually all children come to school with extensive competence with spoken language. They are able to 'read' social situations and come up with what are, for them and members of their families and communities, appropriate openings, comments, silences, questions, responses, endings, etc. Moreover, there is a good deal of evidence which suggests that children's competence is *diglossic*: that is, that they are able to shift styles and types of language and, in the case of bilinguals, from one language to another, to fit the demands of different social situations.

But this is not to say that the speech events they have learned to work within will fit teachers' and schools' very specialised expectations. The school itself forms a specialised culture where there are rules and practices that do not readily occur elsewhere. Later we will consider the highly-patterned rules governing speech events in classrooms, like a group reading lesson or 'morning talk' sessions. But in order to discuss Elsey's case further, we first need to ask whether there is a possible discrepancy between what many children know and can do with language, and what the school expects for academic participation, even in pre-school and year one. This is further compounded when we turn from children's oral language socialisation to their introductions to the practices of literacy.

Literacy as a social construction

To say that literacy is a social construction is to suggest that the possible activities which people undertake with texts of all kinds also are negotiated, constructed, resisted and carried in particular sites in everyday life. Because Western cultures are print-saturated environments, we often take literacy for granted. But literacy is *not* a natural species behaviour. In fact, the use of the alphabet for preserving and retrieving information is only about 24 centuries old, a relatively recent invention in the history of mankind. To this day, some indigenous communities in Africa, South America and Asia operate without the technology of literacy.

Whether in holy books, hand written manuscripts and notes, magazines, laws, ledgers or the internet, text is a social technology – a tool which people have developed and used to interact with, describe and construct their social and physical environments. Indeed, it is a significant tool, one which has proved to be an effective medium for scientific recording and analysis, artisitic expression, government, trade, religion, political organisation and action. It is also a powerful tool which can be used to gain access to culturally-significant knowledge and information. However, it is important to note here that text can also be used negatively – to distort and to bias knowledge and information. As a result, we are increasingly placing a premium on children's development of a *critical literacy* – moving children towards the development of vocabularies and ways of reading and writing that enable them to decode, criticise, contest and transform the texts of dominant social institutions (Muspratt, Luke and Freebody, 1997).

In print cultures, we have come to associate literacy with a range of different uses, not only academic, scientific and economic but also for notetaking, list-making, letter-writing, magazine reading, and even watching television. But both historical and modern cultures have put literacy to work in different ways. Consider the differences between the literacy learned by young Moroccan children and by children of the South Pacific Kiribati Islands. In Morocco, male children learn to recite the Qur'an from memory, beginning this practice from school age. On the island of Tuvalu, one primary use of writing is highly-emotive letter writing, which is an integral part of inter-island and interpersonal communication. So the sites, norms, practices and purposes of *literacy events* – instances of daily interaction around and with text – vary greatly across cultures, stressing different values and ideologies, social actions and interrelationships.

We can extend this perspective to look at the specific ways that children apprentice to literacy in countries like Australia, Canada and the United States. Even within the same geographic areas, there can be a good deal of variety in how children's speech and literacy events are constructed. Examining literacy in the Southern States of America, Heath (1983) found that communities separated only by a few kilometres may present very different childhood socialisations into ways with words and ways with texts. In some communities, for instance, children learned that reading was about sitting still, listening to an authoritative adult reader, and sounding words out when requested. In others, children learned that reading required making unprompted analogies between the stories and events in their daily life. In yet others, oral performance of stories and songs was valued far more than book reading. Not only are these children learning the patterns of oral language in speech events, they are also learning a set of activities and task orientations with literacy: what can be done with texts, which texts are valuable, which texts are taboo, where, what can be said about them, how to interact around them, etc.

The differences that children bring to classrooms, therefore, are not simply individual differences or idiosyncrasies. They are far too patterned to be written off as individual difference. They are the products and constructions of the complex and diverse social learnings from the cultures where children grow, live and interact. These cultures are not just 'traditional' cultures we affiliate with ethnic groups or national origins, but they are best described in terms of the community cultures and sub-cultures where children are socialised. These too, are dynamic and hybrid – mixing, matching and blending traditional values and beliefs, children rearing practices and literacy events with those of new, post-modern popular cultures. So diverse are many community cultures that even to use the term 'mainstream' or 'dominant' culture is deceptive: difference is the norm in post-modern nation states, where more people are crossing borders – physical, geographical, cultural, symbolic and intellectual – than ever before in history. In Australia, which was long defined as a monocultural Anglo-country, over 30 per cent of school children are NESB (non-English-speaking background), with significant numbers of Aboriginal students. These children all engage with popular and globalised cultures. In this context, the idealised Enid Blyton, Brady Bunch, or Janet and John childhoods are irrelevant: the fictions of television and the basal reading series. And just as there is no longer a universal childhood, there is no single pathway to literacy.

Children bring to classrooms differing senses of the rules for using language and text in particular settings. They bring concepts about how to act and interact in speech events and literacy events, some of which match the settings and activities teachers might deem educationally valuable, and others which do not. With these general categories in mind, we return to Elsey, an urban child about to enter a Queensland state school. Here we outline the oral and written practices she will bring to a year one classroom.

A case study

Six-year-old Elsey has lived in the tropical North Queensland city of Townsville (with a population of 100,000) since birth. She and her family are part of the large Torres Strait Islander community which has, since World War II, an increasing presence in Australian mainland centres. In some urban schools, Torres Strait Islanders and Aborigines comprise 10–15 per cent of the primary class student body. Like many members of her community, Elsey is bilingual: she speaks English and Torres Strait Creole (TSC). TSC is the preferred language for everyday communication among many Islanders living on the mainland. While many parents and grandparents might speak traditional languages still used in the islands (for example, Kala Lagaw Ya, Kala Kawaw Ya, Meriam Mir), Elsey and most of her generation speak English and TSC. They are bilingual: switching from English to TSC depending on the particular site and situation for language use. This means that a group of Islanders may use English for a service exchange in a shopping centre, then proceed to use TSC amongst themselves for social exchange, and perhaps a traditional, vernacular language to address elders. This code switching occurs automatically and instantaneously.

TSC is a language which has borrowed and mixed features of phonology, vocabulary, syntax, semantics and pragmatics from traditional languages, English and another hybrid language used across the South Pacific for trade and cross-cultural communication. It is important to note that TSC is not a 'deficient' or 'unsystematic' form of English. It is a rule-governed language, in itself quite capable of meeting the functional demands of its community of speakers in common cultural situations.

Elsey has lived in several different locations over her six years, a reflection of the ongoing problem of finding affordable urban and suburban rented accommodation, and the Islander preference for three- generation family units as a strategy for providing social, emotional and financial support. For some time she lived in the maternal family unit with her mother and grandmother in a two-bedroom flat. By this time she had younger twin sisters. Also living there were her mother's older sister, two adopted children of her grandmother, and a related teenager and primary school-age child. During this period all the school-age children attended nearby schools and Elsey was an avid apprentice during homework sessions. While the older children worked at tables or on the floor, she would call for pencil and paper so that she could also play at doing 'homework'.

For the past year Elsey has lived with her paternal grandmother. From an Islander perspective, this household is unique in one respect: except for rare occasions, neither Elsey's brothers and sisters nor her parents are with her. Grandmother and child share a small, well-maintained maisonette in a fully-integrated urban community. Without other live-in school-age children to accompany Elsey to school, Grandmother decided to place Elsey in a nearby Kindy. In the morning she heads off to the bus, carrying a lunch prepared by Grandmother in her backpack. She calls this backpack her 'letterbox', a reference to the activity sheets, notes and forms she brings home from Kindy. By observing the activities of other Islander children, her Grandmother and family friends, and by participating in Kindy, Elsey is developing a sense of what literacy entails, its artefacts and objects, where it can be used, for what purposes and so forth.

At home Elsey and her grandmother speak TSC most of the time. Elsey chooses to use the English spoken at Kindy when she has commerce outside of the family unit. Elsey is an emergent bilingual. She is already as competent in TSC as other children of her age, and she has learned how to do things with words in the speech events of her culture. This includes knowing how to break into a conversation, when not to interrupt, what is implied by talking 'cheeky', when she must 'tok praply' in more formal settings amongst Islanders, and when pertness and humour are rewarded. At the same time, she is learning English and mainstream Australian culture's rules in speech events with individuals outside her home and immediate circle of relatives. In the following conversations, 'E' stands for Elsey and 'G' for grandmother. Other initials represent other speakers.

E: J. – go'n'get my bloody pencils.
J: Go'n'get your own bloody pencils.
E: J....
J: What?

E: Can you go an' get my pencils, please?

Here Elsey is exploring and learning the protocols for making a request from mainstream English speakers. She often experiments with structures and meanings which achieve her social purposes in a speech situation with TSC speakers. In other situations, family friends and others directly encourage mainstream English patterns:

E: S. – please let go!
Y: Oh, very polite, that!

Often her experimentation with English shows an awareness and developing control of many aspects of how language works.

G: *Wane yu kaikai?* (Wat [do you want to] eat?)
E: Don' know/what I'm gonna eat.
I might be gonna eat' 'ave you got any cornflakes – no/
'ave you got any cornflakes mam?
G: No cornflakes, darling.
E: O.K. I/what we/what're we got? A bread?
Yes, we got a bread.

Elsey already knows a great deal about how English works and, even in this situation which might call upon her to use TSC, she is experimenting with English. She is learning which auxiliaries (might, have) to select; indefinite articles with count and non-count nouns (a loaf of bread, or some bread); rules about how to pose questions; and how to use English pronouns.

We can summarise a number of key points from this brief look at Elsey's oral language use. Elsey is able to do various things with words. Expressing opinions, giving reasons, explaining, challenging, accusing, praising, joking are just some of the social actions she uses language to achieve. But often home speech events take on very different rules and patterns than those that we might expect, understand or even consider 'polite'.

E: [Singing Mary had a little lamb – unsure of pronunciation]
Ma' – laam o lam?
G: [Shrugs shoulders]
E: *O wane yu big fo?* (what good is it you're being an adult?)

For Elsey, the rules governing what can be said to an adult, how to get and hold the floor, who is in control of the speech event are quite distinct from those of the mainstream home and classroom. Further, Elsey shifts from TSC to English and from English to TSC, not randomly but depending on the specific context, the task, the topic, whom she is addressing and other cues. This said, we now turn to the kinds of knowledge and competence with written language which Elsey is developing.

Elsey's Grandmother is marginally literate, having grown up in the Torres Strait when schooling to third grade only was available. She occasionally scans a TSC dictionary and grammar text but she is reluctant to write in either of her languages and her reading is a laborious and uncertain process. Where possible she engages the assistance of clerks and trustworthy relatives and friends to fill out the forms that she, as a pensioner, must contend with. She occasionally receives letters from her daughter on Thursday Island.

Yet Elsey engages with print, often enthusiastically, as part of her daily routines. One of her duties is to clear the mailbox each day, a responsibility she jealously guards. She has learned to recognise the addressee's name on envelopes and she can sometimes identify the logos and acronyms of familiar agencies. As she collected a letter one day, she glanced at the envelope and exclaimed, 'Oh shit, Telecom!', a signal of the significance such bills has in the household. Both she and Grandmother scan and sort the mail daily, with Grandmother directing greeting cards to Elsey: 'Baby, this one is for you!' Elsey eagerly 'reads' cards and letters from brothers, cousins and aunties on Thursday Island, describing what is in them and making up possible stories and tales from the texts she technically might not be able to read.

Elsey, an emergent literate, uses writing and reading for a range of instrumental, recreational, and social interactional purposes (Heath, 1983). She writes her 'name' proudly for Grandmother and herself on scraps of papers, letters and cards; she can also write some close friends' names. For play, she sometimes asks for names and words to be written for her to copy. She sings church songs from books and lyric sheets, often prepared by her Grandmother: 'Mam, you write for me, "Jesus loves me"'. These forms of writing are integrated with leisure-time drawing, making diagrams and simulations of writing: invented spellings and letters which she has developed in imitation of those writers she has observed. What emerges is the kind of composite writing that Dyson (1993) calls 'symbol weaving'. In one early writing/picture, she explained to Joan about her family:

> E. Yeah,
> *dhea, nau ai ken raitem* [subvocalising while writing] (there, now I can write it).
> *Raiting atha pamili neim* (writing other family name).

mai atha pamili neim is... am ... ooh ... now ... oh ... I know ... am ...
ah, mai atha pamili neim is ... Mamali (my other family name is ...
Mamali).
J. Mamali?
E. (louder) Bamali.
J. Bamali?
E. Bob
J. Oh? Bob Marley.

Elsey accompanied this drawing of different letters with a picture of a
man with a Rastafarian hair cut which she referred to as 'a sticky'. This
was her representation of Bob Marley, whose music and folklore figures
prominently among many Islander youth. The sources she draws upon are
varied, including posters she has seen in friends' homes, pictures in flyers
and newspapers, television, radio and music texts. Elsey is using her early
writing as a way of 'naming' herself, her world, and her life – and that life
is a blended, hybrid one that combines images and texts of popular culture
and Torres Strait Islander culture, with those texts that she and
Grandmother must negotiate daily.

Elsey's reading centres on functional print in her environment and she
conceives of reading as serving specific purposes:

J: Are you gonna read the paper or what?
E: Mm?
J: Gonna read the paper?
E: Read the paper for what?

She can recognise names and addresses, and the logos which appear on
signs (e.g., McDonalds, Target). At home, literacy events centre talk
around advertising flyers, newspapers, forms and the texts that she and
her grandmother jointly use. Here Elsey and Grandmother are scanning an
advertising flyer for a local store:

G: Shower curtain, plastic curtain, *yumi gede diswan* (we'll get this
one).
Ai laik diswan (I like this one).
E, tri dola (eh, three dollars).
E: *Jest onli tri dola?*
G: *O, bokli your favrit* (oh, broccoli's your favourite).
E: *En karit mai favrit* (and carrot is my favourite).
G: Celery, not brokli
E: Which one?

G: That wan celery.

E: You think brokli.

G: Mmm... *this backet gud fo Astro* [a dog] *fo slip* (this'd be a good basket for Astro to sleep in).

E: Which basket?

In this and other home literacy events, Elsey is an active participant, responding to Grandmother's prompts, at times switching the focus and topic, and linking the text to her own likes and dislikes, experiences and intentions. She clearly initiates talk and discussion around text and is not the passive recipient of adult-initiated questions or prompts. She and Grandmother switch readily between TSC and English.

Elsey is developing a sense of the social purposes of literacy and interaction patterns around text. Additionally, she is learning technical competences with the technology of text, developing an increasing knowledge of the alphabet, of words she recognises by sight, and of sound/symbol correspondence for attacking unfamiliar words and distinguishing between familiar ones. Yet much of her interaction around the text is bilingual. English remains the primary language of use in mainstream institutions such as commercial organisations, government and schools. Since the TSC vocabulary is largely English-based, only prosodic and phonological (sound) features might signal to a teacher that Elsey may not, at this stage of her language development, be fully a fluent speaker of English.

It is interesting to note – and perhaps crucial to understanding the kinds of problems which Elsey might encounter in her classroom – that most of the functional uses of text and literacy events featured in her home environment do not figure prominently in the early primary school literacy curriculum. Formal school-based introductions to literacy, whether in basal or holistic, skill or process-oriented approaches, tend to emphasise the reading and writing of fictional, narrative texts.

So while Elsey has a knowledge of story forms and events (for example, how to signal beginnings and endings, what counts as a valid story, what can be done by tellers, by listeners, who has the right to speak), it diverges in many ways from the middle-class bedtime story events undertaken in many mainstream homes, eagerly supported by many educators, and emulated in many classrooms. Elsey already can hear and identify cultural differences between stories. At the end of the *Moon Story*, she asks of her Grandmother:

E: Black one?

G: No.

E: Is this a white one?

G: Maybe ... it's just a story.

Elsey here is categorising the cultural bases and sources of stories, already distinguishing those with women and girls who have faces 'jis' like me' as different from those that are 'white'. Not only does the form and content of the Torres Strait stories stand apart from that of conventional children's literature (whether Golden Books or award winners), but storytelling is an oral performance with very different roles, expectations and rules. The crocodile story at the beginning of this chapter is the beginning of an extended story in which Elsey used a range of literary and narrative devices, some of which she has acquired from her Grandmother's stories.

Another key environment for Elsey's language socialisation is interaction with the spoken and visual texts of radio and television. Elsey and her Grandmother like to listen to a local commercial radio station which broadcasts popular and rock music, and features a high-profile local announcer who mixes local news, sports, birthday calls and competitive phone in quizzes with advertisements from local businesses. Elsey knows the lyrics and melodies of dozens of rock songs, often dancing and singing in chorus with the songs when they come on the radio. The following conversation illustrates how she interacts with the announcer, music and radio.

E: Let's do the time! [switches on radio to check the time].

Thank you, Mam

'Thank you Mister 'ooker!' [quotes L.J. Hooker real estate advertisement].

E: Anyway, I need to ... listen to one of my favourite song.

G: [unintelligible, radio announces local 'Sky Show'].

E: Mama!

I go go Sky Show!

the Sky show is coming

ai go tel yu dhe (I'll tell you about it).

G: Wha?

E: I bin gad Sky Show dhe we yu go kam daun iya (the Sky show was there where you go down the hill).

G: True?

E: Yeah, iya spik/ and I/ and dem/wiskain dem polisman go do (they're talking about/ and 'e/ and they/ the police are going to do something I think).

Hey I friend all my life for you [singing along with song by Linda Ronstadt and Aaron Neville].

Here Elsey is talking with Grandmother around the radio text, in effect translating the broadcaster's comments into TSC for Grandmother, shifting codes fluidly and continuously. As she often does, she breaks back into song, accurately reproducing the phrasing and dialect of the popular songs she likes so much. This kind of diglossic behaviour requires fluency and excellent listening skills; in Elsey's case, frequently developed around the texts of popular culture.

We have here provided a necessarily brief sketch of Elsey's language and literate development. However, we can make several pertinent observations about her language and literacy when she enters her year one classroom. Elsey is bilingual, fully fluent for her age in TSC and with a growing functional vocabulary and a developing competence in English. Her language and knowledge of speech events in TSC with other Islanders is adequate for her community and family needs. She can achieve a wide range of social and intellectual goals with TSC. As we have illustrated, she is rapidly acquiring a better knowledge of how to use English appropriately in different sites and situations. Much of this development will depend on continuing opportunities to experiment with language in speech events with mainstream speakers of English. With family friends and acquaintances, she is encouraged in her use of English and her switching to TSC is not met with hostility or misunderstanding.

Elsey also is engaged with the texts of mainstream popular, commercial and institutional cultures, which provide rich sources for her developing reading, writing and oral language patterns. She interacts with spoken, visual and written media texts daily – rehearsing language patterns from television and radio, from music and commercials with great finesse and creativity. From these texts she is stitching together a social identity (Hall, 1996) – one that combines her knowledge of traditional values and stories from her Grandmother, with heroes and imagery from popular music and culture. If we are to understand and engage with her cultural background and practices, we must attend to these blendings and hybridisations of popular culture, mainstream everyday texts and traditional practices and sources of knowledge, and not rely on the anthropological stereotypes of indigenous and migrant cultures that are frequently presented to educators.

Finally, Elsey has developed a seminal knowledge about literacy. She participates in various literacy events at home and at Kindy, from playing 'homework' and copying words, to 'reading' signs, newspapers, advertisements. She can write strings of letters and has a sense that this is a way of coding words, sounds and meanings. She often combines these 'words' with her drawings. Further, she has developed a facility at 'yarning' in both TSC and English, participating with Grandmother in the oral performance of Islander stories and recounting events in which she has had a role. Diverse intercultural texts and resources are at play in her life: but not the conventional texts of children's literature that feature prominently in many middle-class Anglo childhoods, often defined as the precursors of literacy.

We hope that when she enters a year one classroom next year, she will encounter a supportive environment which will recognise her developing facilities with language and literacy and use them as stepping stones towards the kinds of competence that she will need to succeed in school. But there are bound to be problems. We conclude by outlining some possible scenarios for Elsey and by turning to larger questions about language and literacy, difference and power which warrant further attention.

Literacy, equity and power

What will happen when Elsey enters the mainstream classroom in a few months time? How will her fluency in TSC and developing competence in English, her knowledge of literacy events, fit with the following kind of classroom literacy event? This is a 'reading around the group' session from an Australian year one class working with a standardised reading textbook series (Baker and Freebody, 1989, p.167):

T: Why is it [the train] getting slower and slower, and slower?
S: Because it's a real steep hill and the carriages might fall off?
T: It's a very, very steep hill, yes. [Resumes reading].
S: He must be strong.
T: Yes he must be! [Resumes reading].
   Who knows why they have tunnels for trains to go through?
S: To keep them out of the rain.
T: Does rain hurt trains? Jack?
S: To go through big hills.
T: Yes, that's right. If you have a big hill like that...

We present this lesson not as a template to follow, but as an example of the kinds of talk around text which occur in early literacy programmes. Various unstated rules are at work here: the teacher asks questions, students answer, usually in brief clauses; the teacher nominates the book for study, the topics for discussion, and who will speak when, about what; she defines what will count as a valid answer. Many Australian early childhood teachers emphasise discussions of character motivation, pictorial features, and plot prediction; others focus more on language features of the texts. Most literacy lessons focus on this kind of simplified textbook narratives rather than the kinds of functional, popular or multimedia texts that figure in Elsey's world. School-based book reading is about participating in these kinds of literacy events: about getting the floor, guessing what the teacher wants to know about the story and what is an accurate 'reading'. We will not discuss here whether this is a quality lesson. Our point is that these kinds of lessons become the norm of our teaching. Their rules and patterns may systematically exclude children like Elsey from showing what they know and can do with language.

We can only speculate on Elsey's transition from the speech and literacy events of home to those of the classroom. Our point is that particular approaches to literacy in the school systematically favour those children whose previous language and literate socialisation has accustomed them to rules and procedures of the classroom literacy event. Inversely, these same approaches may systematically work against those children whose previous language and literate socialisation has taught them other rules and procedures for speech and literacy events. As sociologists have argued, schools have a way of valorising and rewarding those children who bring to classrooms what teachers expect of them (Bourdieu and Passeron, 1977). We have made the case here that Elsey does not have any intrinsic 'lack' or 'deficit'. But unless we are able to reconstruct and shape our classroom literacy materials and events to fit what she knows and can do, we may set out the conditions for her to fail even before she begins.

Judging by the data on school achievement of indigenous and culturally different children, the prognosis for children like Elsey is not good. At present, urban Torres Strait Islander children do not perform as well in conventional schools as their mainstream counterparts (Kale, 1990); neither do children of non-English speaking migrant backgrounds. We believe the problem is at least, partly due to:

• A mismatch between speech and literacy events of the community/home and those of the school.
• Mainstream schools' inability to recognise and capitalise on those knowledges and practices, texts and discourses – including those of popular culture – that children bring to school.
• Schools' and programmes' inability to provide explicit and scaffolded introductions to the kinds of specialised English language and literacy required in a range of academic and community contexts.

There are constructive ways of breaking this pattern that many teachers have already put to effective use. Heath (1983) engaged primary and secondary teachers in the study of community ways with words and texts to increase recognition of what was expected of their students outside of the classroom in community and occupational settings. Further, by making these community patterns the object of classroom study, and by sending children out to gather data on how language was used in the community, teachers were able to provide scaffolded language activities and instruction which enabled a more successful transition to the specialised texts, genres and events of school literacy. In work with Hawaiian children, members of the Kamehameha Early Childhood project redesigned early reading lessons, such as the one described earlier, to better fit those speech events to which Hawaiian children were accustomed at home and in the community. Reading comprehension and achievement improved markedly (Au and Jordan, 1981). Finally, in work with bilingual Hispanic students, Edelsky (1996) and colleagues developed a range of holistic instructional approaches which stressed learners' responsibility for their talk and writing, resulting in improved achievement and the enhancement of their capacity to talk about texts critically.

In Australia, Brian Gray (1984) and colleagues at Traeger Park school in the Northern Territory developed strategies for introducing Aboriginal children of non-English speaking backgrounds to specialised uses of English in particular speech and literacy events. The task, as Gray saw it, was to engage children's first language competence and learning strategies in the classroom mastery of English. 'Concentrated language encounters' were built around meaningful shared themes and events (such as 'saddling a horse', 'going to the pet shop'). These classroom scaffolds were used to elicit and engage a range of characteristic oral and written texts as they might occur in real speech and literacy events, and to do so in a way which stressed the children's capacity to negotiate meanings based on their shared understanding of the situation, information and task at hand.

Literacy is never a stand-alone classroom phenomenon, a simple question of finding the correct pedagogy, curriculum or individual psychology. School literacy instruction is an institutional practice always embedded in community matters of cultural identity, economic access and social power. Much sociological research indicates that education systems produce inequality by disbursing competence and knowledge unequally to children of different social groups. There is ample evidence that literacy teaching and learning in schools play a key role in this cycle. Children enter school with various kinds and levels of oral and literate knowledge and competences. These in turn are validated, cancelled and privileged by schools which often reward those with the most mainstream, school-like competence. In effect, not all children gain equal chances towards powerful literacies. Success and failure in school achievement, and access to well paying jobs and tertiary institutions throughout Western countries, continue to fall along the historical fault lines of class, race and gender.

As Kalantzis, Cope and Slade (1989) have pointed out, programmes which simply aim to celebrate and tolerate cultural and linguistic differences – the 'pizza and spaghetti' approach to multiculturalism – too often fail to address systematically-existing inequities in access to cultural power and economic resources, and indeed language and literacy. At present – the best intentions and hard work of many teachers notwithstanding – schools and programmes are not doing a fully effective job of ensuring that *all* children, regardless of their cultural and class backgrounds, have equal opportunities to engage with powerful literacies. That this disadvantage begins in children's earliest experiences of schooling provides an imperative and a challenge for us all. We have tried here to show a way forward that begins from the teacher's ability to engage in a critical reading of the differences that children like Elsey bring to the classroom. From these understandings, we can begin to open out the possibilities not only for Elsey to use language and literacy to transform her world and her community, but also to provide strategies that encourage her to work with us to transform the ways that we work in our classrooms.

Acknowledgements

This case study was supported by the Australian Research Council. A more extended discussion of aspects of methodology and data is undertaken in Kale (1995). We thank Elsey and her family, and members of the Torres Strait Islander community, for their support and encouragement, Shirley Brice-Heath for advice on data collection, and Courtney Cazden for comments on the analysis.

References

Au, K.H. and Jordan, C. (1981) 'Teaching Reading to Hawaiian Children: Finding a culturally appropriate solution', in Trueba, H., Guthrie, G., and Au, K.H. (Eds). *Culture and the Bilingual Classroom*. Rowley, MA: Newbury House.

Baker, C.D. and Freebody, P. (1989) *Children's First School Books*. Oxford: Basil Blackwell.

Bourdieu, P. and Passeron, J.C. (1977) *Reproduction in Education, Society and Culture*. R. Nice (Trans.). London: Sage.

Buckingham, D. and Sefton-Green, J. (1995) *Cultural Studies Goes to School*. London: Taylor and Francis

Dyson, A.H. (1993) *The Social Worlds of Children Learning to Write in an Urban Primary School*. New York: Teachers College Press.

Edelsky, C. (1996) *With Literacy and Justice for All*, 2nd edition. London: Taylor and Francis.

Gee, J.P. (1996) *Social Linguistics and Literacies*, 2nd edition. London: Taylor and Francis.

Gray, B. (1984) *Helping Children to Become Language Learners in the Classroom*. Darwin: Northern Territory Department of Education.

Hall, S. (1996), 'Introduction: Who Needs "Identity"?' in S. Hall and P. du Gay, (Eds) *Questions of Cultural Identity*. London: Sage.

Heath, S.B. (1983) *Ways with Words*. Cambridge: Cambridge University Press.

Kalantzis, M., Cope, B. and Slade, D. (1989) *Minority Languages and Dominant Culture*. London: Falmer Press.

Kale, J. (1995) *'Ai Gad Dha Pawa': Practices of orality and literacy of an urban Torres Strait Islander child*. Unpublished PhD dissertation, James Cook University of North Queensland, Townsville, Queensland, Australia.

Kale, J. (1990) 'Controllers or Victims: Language and Education in the Torres Strait', in Baldauf, R. and Luke, A. (Eds) *Language Planning and Education in Australasia and the South Pacific*. Clevedon: Multilingual Matters.

Kress, G. (1989) *Linguistic Processes in Sociocultural Practice*, 2nd edition. Oxford: Oxford University Press.

Luke, A. (1994) *The Social Construction of Literacy in the Primary Classroom*. Melbourne: Macmillan.

Muspratt, S., Luke, A. and Freebody, P. (Eds) (1997) *Constructing Critical Literacies*. Creskill, NJ/Sydney: Hampton Press/Allen & Unwin.

Part II

Up to Five: Learning to Live With Different Languages

In Part Two, we learn more about the knowledge and skills acquired by young emergent bilinguals in their homes in Britain, Germany and the USA. The authors then go on to show that what happens to these skills as the children begin pre-school will depend on both the parameters set by educational provision in each country *and* the teacher's own knowledge and awareness. The crucial question is: 'How can very young children gain a sense of "belonging" when they enter a new and very strange environment?' Each author stresses the importance of different mediators of the language and learning practices of the classroom: bilingual assistants, teachers, parents, siblings, films and videos. Mediators promote continuity of language and learning whilst introducing children to the rules of participation in school. How does this take place? Finely-tuned analyses of classroom interaction reveal a syncretism – a blending of home and school language and learning practices. Examples of this occur during activities such as doing sums with siblings, writing with parents, watching dual-language videos at school and home, and discussing special cultural occasions with bilingual assistants. Above all, the children themselves call upon their different worlds as they experiment together during socio-dramatic play in the classroom. The themes of fantasy and play, language and literacy mediators and syncretism all continue into Part Three of this book.

Chapter 3

Two sisters at school: issues for educators of young bilingual children

Rose Drury

Introduction

> Nazma enters nursery with her mother, holding her sister Yasmin's hand. They join the class on the carpet and Yasmin (aged four and a half) finds their names. They sit down together, holding hands. Mrs Raja comes into nursery and takes a group of Pahari speakers for a small group activity. Nazma listens to the story of *The Very Hungry Caterpillar*, told in Pahari. She watches, but does not participate. The children go outside to play. She sits on the rocking boat with Yasmin and two other girls, and then holds Mrs Raja's hand near the climbing frame. After drink time on the carpet, she is directed to the drawing table with Yasmin and Mrs Raja. She attempts to trace over her name and then goes into the book corner on her own. She takes a book and shows it to a nursery nurse. There is no verbal response. She walks over to the sand tray, sucking her fingers, and plays on her own. She spends a few moments at the gluing table and at the threading activity. Mrs Raja is in the book corner and she joins her. Nazma talks to her about the pictures of fruit in Pahari. It is tidy-up time and the children sit on the carpet for a story. Nazma sits next to her sister and watches. Their mother appears at the door and they go home.

Nazma is nearly four years old. Her mother tongue is Pahari (a Panjabi dialect spoken by people originating from the Khotli area of Azad Kashmir, which borders north-east Pakistan). She has been at nursery in Britain for seven weeks. At first, none of the monolingual nursery staff talk to Nazma (except for classroom management purposes) and there is no verbal interaction with other children in the nursery (apart from her sister). The only member of staff she is able to understand, and with whom she can communicate, is the bilingual classroom assistant (Mrs Raja).

Naseem is Nazma's elder sister, the second oldest child in the family. She is nine years old and in a year four class at the same school.

The session starts with a whole-class discussion about geography work on the British Isles. Naseem sits with a group of friends, passive and disengaged. The class then return to their desks and continue the on-going classwork which was introduced earlier in the week. The task is to complete a worksheet on the countries in the British Isles, to calculate the area of each using squared paper and to answer a set of questions about the map. Most of the children in the class are working in pairs or small groups, but Naseem is sitting on her own. She has been working on this worksheet for several days, but is still counting the small squares on the map surface of each country and finding the task difficult. During the session, she is easily distracted and off task for much of the time. She sits for long periods of time not engaged in the work and not asking for help from the classteacher or her peers. Later in the afternoon session when tackling the worksheet, it is evident that the question 'how many times bigger than Northern Ireland is the Republic of Ireland?' is difficult for her to understand. She sits at her desk with her hand held up, asking for help. After several minutes the class teacher asks the class to tidy up. The children assemble on the carpet at the end of the afternoon and go home.

A principal aim of education in every country is to establish parameters within which teachers carry out their professional role, children learn and parents support their children's learning. These parameters are established through custom and tradition, legislation, policy at national, local and school levels, and the preferred style of class teachers as they demonstrate what counts as learning in classrooms. They amount to the norm which children come to understand, and they are often taken for granted by both teachers and children. The norm includes appropriate ways of behaving, styles of learning, ways of speaking and interacting with others, and the understanding and acceptance of teacher expectations. They are all likely to be products of the dominant culture from which assumptions about language use and common values in education are drawn. Children like Nazma and Naseem present a challenge to schools because their language use, and their socialisation and cultural experience in and beyond the home, does not match the norm which teachers expect to be able to build on.

The nursery context which Nazma experiences is based on an established tradition of 'good practice' in early years education. This is derived from a 'child-centred' approach to teaching and learning. It is strongly influenced by the philosophy of education which informed the Plowden Report (1967). This is still widely endorsed by early years practitioners. Although this approach is an 'inclusive' one, the difficulty for the nursery teacher is how to ensure that Nazma's home and linguistic experience is understood and taken into account within the classroom norms.

In this chapter, I contrast the home and school learning of these two sisters, and discuss ways in which the parameters might be widened to enable children at an early stage in their learning of an additional language to achieve as well as those children whose language and experience conform more closely to what is expected.

Learning at home

Nazma and Naseem's family originated from the Khotli area of Azad Kashmir, although they subsequently moved to Gujarat. Their father's family came to Watford, near London, in the 1960s, at a time when workers were needed in the local factories and remained in Britain. Their father attended the same primary school as Nazma and Naseem, stayed at school until he was 16, but gained no qualifications. Their mother, Khurshid, arrived in the early 1970s, attended primary school for a short while and returned to Pakistan. She attended primary school in Pakistan and remained there until her marriage to Nazeem's father, who brought her back to England. They returned to Watford and lived in the family house. There are six children in the family, and Nazma and Naseem's early socialisation was centred at home with their parents, grandmother and siblings. The children all attend the same nursery and primary school. The role of their grandmothers (one lives in their house and one lives nearby) is significant in the family context, particularly in the development of their mother tongue. Their grandmother has a close relationship with the children, spends time talking to them in the home and telling them stories from her childhood.

Nazma uses her mother tongue, Pahari, with all members of the family. The older school-age children use English more to communicate with each other at home. Their mother always speaks Pahari to her children and is proud of the fact that they are all fluent in their mother tongue. She tells them stories she remembers from her childhood, drawing on an oral tradition which is not recorded in written form. She would like to see them grow up speaking two languages and hopes that they will maintain their

Pahari, despite the change to English when they enter school. The close links with their extended family, the presence of grandmother in the home and the satellite television channel (ZEE TV), which is watched for considerable periods of time during the day and includes films in Panjabi and songs in Urdu, all promote the continuing use of the mother tongue at home.

The older children attend Qur'anic classes after school and all members of the family recite verses and prayers in Arabic, and read the Arabic primers and holy Qur'an at home. Zakkia (the eldest child, 11 years old) has completed the task of reading of the Qur'an, and Yasmin and Nazma will begin when they are about five years old. Their mother would like them also to learn Urdu (the official language of literacy in Pakistan) from a young age, but a local class is not available and Urdu is not taught at school.

Naseem shares responsibilities with her older sister, Zakkia, helping their mother with the younger children and the housework. Her mother thinks that she is doing very well at school. She reads letters and explains the school newsletter to her, writes shopping lists, takes her shopping, and helps at the doctors. Naseem brings books home from school to read. Her mother thinks she reads and writes well and that she asks a wide range of questions. After school, she attends Qur'anic classes and she also reads the Arabic verses with her mother at home. Her mother has no contact with the school but the reports say that Naseem's work is satisfactory. Although her mother is unable to communicate with the school, she says, 'If I were educated and knew what was going on in the school, I would go and discuss it; as this is not the case, I am relying on the school to let me know.'

Nazma (the youngest child) has not attended a playgroup or any other pre-school setting, but her early-learning experiences have focused on playing with her siblings, particularly Yasmin, and other members of the extended family who visit frequently. Nazma talks fluently to her siblings in her mother tongue (Pahari) and takes part in role play and dressing-up activities. She also watches, helps and talks to her mother when working in the house. She particularly enjoys sorting the clothes and helping to prepare and cook food at home. Her mother sees her as 'brighter' than the others in the family because of the way she thinks and behaves in the home setting. She has high aspirations for her daughter and expects her to achieve well in the education system.

Nazma, then, has a rich family life with daily contacts with five older siblings, parents and grandparents. Religion is of great significance in her home and it is understood that attendance at Qur'anic classes is expected.

Religious and cultural values are conveyed through family conversation, the stories she hears and her contacts with parents and grandparents. These are central to her cognitive and language development also. At the same time, her home life includes the use of English, although she does not yet use this language herself, and she will be increasingly aware of the biculturalism that her older brothers and sisters are acquiring through their schooling and through television. She is fully occupied with learning in the home context, and she is encouraged to participate as a member of the family in many ways. But these are not necessarily ways that will prepare her for the expectations in a British nursery setting. For example, she is not encouraged to draw and paint, she does not have bedtime stories read to her, she does not play with construction toys, and she is not used to being asked what she thinks about a topic. Yet such activities and responses will be central to the culture of her nursery. The description of Nazma opening this chapter showed her in the midst of just such a context.

Naseem learning at school

The primary school Naseem, Nazma and their siblings attend has 270 pupils in all (including a 60 place nursery unit) and approximately 40 per cent are of ethnic minority background. Thirty per cent of the pupils are bilingual, their families mainly originate from Azad Kashmir and share the same mother tongue, Pahari.

Naseem has attended the school from nursery to year four. It is evident from her response to the geography lesson described above that she is struggling with the demands of the curriculum. The task requires an understanding of content (a knowledge of the countries in the British Isles); linguistic skills (how many times bigger than Northern Ireland is the Republic of Ireland) and mathematical skills (calculating the area of the map surface). The way that conceptualising problems may be closely related to English-language development is illustrated through her difficulty in understanding the question about the relative size of Northern Ireland and the Republic of Ireland. Naseem is aware of the difficulties she has with her school work. She does not understand the classwork and says, 'I get shy sometimes [in the whole class context] and I don't know what to say because I might be wrong.' She has developed strategies to disengage from the classroom tasks and, as exemplified in the passage, she does not interact with the class teacher or her peers. At this stage, she knows that she is having little success, she is able to acknowledge that she needs help, yet she lacks the confidence to be proactive about helping herself. The attempt to engage in the task (part of the now stronger expected parameters of the year four classroom), the limited understanding, the partial disengagement, the inability to ask for help, and the resulting failure to complete the task are all part of a familiar cycle to Naseem. Her perception of herself as a learner is poor.

Naseem's class teacher sees her as underachieving in all areas of the curriculum. He says that she has no self-belief, lacks confidence and is convinced that she cannot do the classwork. She does not ask for help and needs a great deal of support in class. Her class teacher sees that she can achieve some success with her work if she has sufficient repetition and visual clues, as well as additional support from second-language support staff, though he feels she will sink in a secondary school. He has no contact at all with her parents and he has no evidence of their support for her learning at school.

How might we explain Naseem's problems at school in contrast with her learning at home? The example from her geography lesson highlights three areas of difficulty.

1. There is clearly a mismatch between the experiences, expectations and views of her achievement at home and at school. Perhaps the most pointed and unnecessary aspect of this mismatch is that the school appears to have misled Naseem's parents about her level of achievement.
2. She is struggling with the demands of the curriculum as she is still acquiring English for academic purposes.
3. Naseem's difficulties may partially be explained by her inability to use her mother tongue as a means of access to new and complex concepts presented in class.

As Nazma steps into school, the crucial question will be: 'how far will Nazma's experiences be different from those of her sister?' With each of these aspects in mind, we turn to examine more closely Nazma's prospects as she enters nursery.

Nazma learning at school

English language development

The following transcript – the teacher is talking about caterpillars in the classroom – reflects a typical afternoon 'carpet time' nursery session. There are five other Pahari-speaking children attending nursery (including her sister, Yasmin, and her cousin, Hassan) and they are all at an early stage in their learning of English. The nursery has an established routine which is followed every day. The children sit on the large carpet with the nursery teacher at the beginning of the session. Nazma is present but silent.

Teacher:	Remember how we started off?
Children:	Yes [altogether].
Teacher:	It wasn't a caterpillar to begin with, was he?
Child A:	He started to go out the egg.
Teacher:	Yes, he started out of just a little egg on the leaf and that's how our caterpillars started. We didn't see them as eggs, we only had them as little caterpillars, but they started as eggs and then hatched out into caterpillars. This afternoon I want you to do a picture from the story. So, what do you think you could draw from the story?
Child B:	I'm drawing a butterfly.
Teacher:	Yes, you could draw a butterfly, couldn't you?
Child C:	I'm going to do the egg.
Child D:	I'm going to do the food.
Teacher:	Yes, you could draw the caterpillar eating all the food. Yes, you could draw the little egg on the leaf.
Child C:	The caterpillar out the egg.
Teacher:	When he?
Child C:	He came out the egg.
Teacher:	When he hatched out of the egg and out popped the little hungry caterpillar. 'Cos caterpillars really...
Child C:	I'm going to draw egg.
Teacher:	What do they really eat?
Children:	Leaves.
Teacher:	Leaves, don't they. They don't really eat lollipops and strawberries and cupcakes. They like to eat leaves. So you can draw anything you like from the story.

In this example we can see some of the implicit turn-taking rules and language 'recipes' (Hymes, 1974) which the children are expected to understand and follow in the nursery classroom. Firstly, the teacher does much of the talking, directs the discussion, selects the choice of topic, asks the questions, shows approval and repeats 'correct' answers. The teacher's use of language is aimed at a level appropriate for children who are native English speakers (for example, 'out popped the little hungry caterpillar'). Linguistically, the task is also a complex one. Nazma is expected to be familiar with the lexical set of 'caterpillar' which here includes 'egg', 'butterfly', 'leaf', 'hatch', with past and present tenses (came, like) and with modal verbs (could). Secondly, the children sit and listen, make appropriate comments, answer questions briefly and put up their hands when they want to speak. These routines have been rehearsed many times by most of the children in the nursery, but Nazma has not yet learnt the rules, cultural practices and expectations. In addition, at present she does not have the English language skills to understand or engage in the classroom discussion. She sits silently, observing and listening. From such interactions we can see how difficult it might be to unpick and learn the rules of participation.

Yet, little attention has been given to the learning of young bilingual children like Nazma who are at an early stage in their learning English as an additional language in Britain. There has also been a lack of informed guidance for teachers working with bilingual children in the pre-school years. In addition, there has been an assumption, influenced by Krashen's (1982) emphasis on exposure to 'comprehensible input', that the acquisition of English as an additional language in these settings will take place 'naturally'. But, as is now evident in Naseem's situation, not all children are able to acquire the English required for school learning purposes during these early years.

Nazma's nursery teacher thinks that her English will progress in 'leaps and bounds'. However, Naseem's underachievement in the education system shows us that this might not be the case. The OfSTED report into the achievement of ethnic minority pupils found that 'the lower average attainments of Bangladeshi and Pakistani pupils in the early key stages may reflect the significance of levels of fluency in English, which are strongly associated with performance at this stage.' (OfSTED, 1996: 1) Nazma's silence supports research on teacher/pupil interaction, showing that teachers in primary classrooms interacted less frequently with minority ethnic children (Biggs and Edwards, 1992). In this context, Nazma's prospects may not be as encouraging as her teacher's optimism suggests.

Paying close attention to Nazma's English language development will address one key area of her learning needs. However, the remaining aspects are equally important. First, her cognitive development at this stage is crucially dependent on the use and extension of her mother tongue. Second, Nazma's learning requires support through home–school understandings. There is a need to expand the parameters of multi-lingual classrooms to include the following:

• An informed knowledge by all staff of second/additional language

development for young children.
- Planning to exploit language development opportunities in all nursery activities.
- Planned and consistent inclusion in small group activities which enable the bilingual child both to interact with peers and to use language which has been modelled by the teacher.
- Frequent opportunities for interaction with the teacher who uses sensitive questioning techniques to enable the child to engage with the activity.
- Planned monitoring and discussion so that reinforcing or extending new language can be included in planning.

Mother tongue development

Contrast the previous example with this interaction between Mrs Raja and Nazma as they discuss a counting book in Pahari.

Mrs Raja:	What's this?
Nazma:	Apples.
Mrs Raja:	What's this?
Nazma:	Pears.
Mrs Raja:	What's this?
Nazma:	Lemon, yuk I don't like that [making a face].
Mrs Raja:	Don't you like it, because it's sour?
Nazma:	Yes.
Mrs Raja & Nazma:	1,2,3 green apples [counting together].
Mrs Raja & Nazma:	1,2,3,4 pears [counting together].
Nazma:	We eat them, we like them, we get them, we go to a shop and we buy apples and pears...
Nazma:	We went to the shops with mum and Hasnan and we bought lollies. We had Hasnan's birthday. We went in a big 'mosque' and there were lots of people, [the 'mosque' is in fact a hall]. Friends and everybody there. There was cake. I went with Hasnan to the shops.

Nazma:	Mum came [to the party], everybody came.
Nazma:	I saw a cat and I was crying when I saw a cat, it was coming to hurt me.
Mrs Raja:	What did mum do?
Nazma:	She said cat go away.
	Then we ate, Yasmin and Hasnan were eating, and grandma was crying.
Mrs Raja:	Why?
Nazma:	Because it was hurting.
	We went to mosque.
	Lots of people were there.
	Mum was crying and everybody was crying.

This transcript is very different from the previous example in the nursery. The conversation with Nazma is embedded in her family, culture and religion and illustrates the importance of building on home experiences. From the extract, a number of observations can be made. First, the opportunity to sit and look at a book with Mrs Raja provides the appropriate context for Nazma to relate a story from her home experience at length. She talks about significant events in her life, knowing that Mrs Raja will understand. Her grandmother is crying because she is unwell and this leads her to talk about going to the mosque during the Muslim month of Muharram. During the first 10 days of this month every evening, Nazma and her family, who are Shia Muslims, visit the mosque, listen to the story of the suffering experienced at a particular point of Islamic history and show their respect and sadness.

Second, Nazma knows that Mrs Raja will be able to interpret the meaning of her stories and she is able to express her thoughts and extend her mother tongue use. Nazma knows the names of different fruits in her mother tongue and speaks very clearly and fluently about her home experiences. The crucial role of bilingual staff is highlighted here as this is the only occasion during the nursery session when Nazma is able to talk and begin to make sense of the 'strange world' she has entered.

In Britain there has been very little research into bilingual education and young bilingual children, except for the Mother Tongue English Teaching (MOTET) project (Fitzpatrick, 1987). We know, however, from research evidence elsewhere, that children benefit from bilingual education. In Canada, for example, Swain and Cummins (1979:14) found that:

Specifically when the home language is different from the school language and the home language tends to be denigrated by others and themselves, and where the children come from socio-economically deprived homes, it would appear appropriate to begin instruction in the child's first language, switching at a later stage to instruction in the school language.

In a major study in the United States known as the National Association for Bilingual Education No-Cost Study (NNCS), the main finding of Rodriguez and his colleagues (Rodriguez et al, 1995:489) is that 'the cognitive impact of a bilingual pre-school experience on the bilingual language development of language minority children is positive in nature.' From the evidence of the extract of Nazma talking with Mrs Raja, this comment would appear to be equally valid in Britain. We must include a planned approach to mother tongue support if we seriously wish to enhance Nazma's cognitive development.

Home–school understandings

The interaction between Nazma and Mrs Raja shows clearly the unique position of the bilingual classroom assistant to mediate the new language and culture for Nazma. Nazma's language and knowledge of speech events in Pahari is adequate for her community and family needs, yet when she enters nursery she does not have the necessary skills to engage with the learning experiences. We have also seen that Nazma and her siblings are 'active participants' in a range of activities at home, but these resources, or 'funds of knowledge' (Moll et al, 1992) of the child's world outside the classroom are rarely drawn on at school.

There are a number of studies which document the difficulties experienced by children from 'non-mainstream' backgrounds when there is a mismatch between home and school cultural practices (Heath, 1983; Michaels, 1986; Gregory, 1993). Rogoff (1993) studied toddlers and their care-givers in Guatemala and the United States, and their 'guided participation' in different cultural activities. She found that children from a variety of communities, with different socialisation practices, all appear to have in common opportunites to learn, but variations across communities included differences in the 'goals of development and the nature of involvement of children and adults' (Rogoff:249). In her work on the early socialisation of two different communities in the United States, Heath (1983:343) considers 'how teachers' knowledge of children's ways enabled them to bring these ways into their classrooms.' In Arizona, Moll has developed a project that is studying household and classroom practices in Mexican communities. In this project, teachers visited homes to find out about the 'funds of knowledge' children bring to school. This work led to in-service training and the development of appropriate teaching programmes.

We have seen that bilingual staff have an important role in helping mediate a continuity between the cultural and linguistic expectations of both home and school. Mrs Raja is able to bridge the gap between experiences in the home and those within the nursery. She uses her mother tongue for learning purposes in the nursery, talks to Nazma about her home experiences and communicates with parents. As the research studies in the United States have indicated, it is evident that all nursery staff need to take steps to understand better children's home experiences in order to plan for teaching. At the same time, there is a need for more extensive, organised and planned use of bilingual staff, which fits in with and extends the nursery practice.

Ways ahead

In this chapter the experience of Nazma and Naseem has been examined in the context of the expectations in classroom settings, current guidance for nursery practice, and research findings. If we are to fulfil the recent promise made for equal opportunities in the School Curriculum and Assessment Authority (SCAA) document, *Desirable Outcomes for Children's Learning,* that educators of four year olds should 'provide a framework for planning educational activities which ensure equality of opportunity, based on children's previous experience and achievement, and respond to individual needs' (SCAA, 1996:1), policy makers and those concerned with initial and in-service training will have to address five issues.

1. They must recognise the importance of education which takes place in the mother tongue and build on children's developing linguistic and cognitive competences as they enter nursery.
2. They will have to ensure there is a better understanding of children's home experiences in order to build on these when planning for learning in the nursery.
3. They must allow for a more extensive and planned use of bilingual staff to mediate between home and school and to extend nursery practice.
4. They will have to provide explicit and detailed guidance for teachers working with young children learning English as an additional language.

5. They must give opportunities for research into the areas of second language development, teacher–child interaction, bilingual approaches (including the work of bilingual classroom assistants) and school/community partnerships to inform practitioners working in the early years.

Naseem and Nazma highlight the challenges facing all those involved in the educational provision for children learning English as an additional language in Britain. Only when we respond to these challenges will we be able to provide access to the equal opportunities we promise to them and which they deserve.

Acknowledgements

I would like to thank all the school staff involved in this study for their generosity and patience, Mussarat Fazal for her invaluable help, interpretation and transcription of the recorded data and, above all, for the Shah family's involvement in the project.

References

Biggs, A. and Edwards, V. (1994) 'I treat them all the same: Teacher–pupil talk in multiethnic classrooms', in Graddol, D., Maybin, J. and Stierer, B. (Eds) *Researching Language and Literacy in Social Context*. Clevedon: Multilingual Matters.

Central Advisory Council for Education (1967) *Children and their Primary Schools (The Plowden Report)*. London: HMSO.

Dulay, H., Burt, M. and Krashen, S. (1982) *Language Two*. Oxford: Oxford University Press.

Fitzpatrick, B. (1987) *The Open Door*. Clevedon: Multilingual Matters.

Gregory, E. (1993) 'Sweet and Sour: Learning to read in a British and Chinese school', *English in Education*, **27** (3), 53–9.

Heath, S.B. (1983) *Ways with Words: Language, life and work in communities and classrooms*. Cambridge: Cambridge University Press.

Hymes, D. (1974) *Foundations in Sociolinguistics*. Philadelphia: University of Philadelphia Press.

Michaels, S. (1986) 'Narrative Presentations: An oral preparation for literacy with first graders', in Cook-Gumperz, J. (Ed.) *The Social Construction of Literacy*. Cambridge: Cambridge University Press.

Moll, L. *et al.* (1992) 'Funds of Knowledge for Teaching: Using a qualitative approach to connect homes and classrooms', *Theory Into Practice*, **31** (2), 132–41.

OfSTED (1996) *Recent Research on the Achievements of Ethnic Minority Pupils*. London: HMSO.

Rodriguez, J. *et al.* (1995) 'The Impact of Bilingual Preschool Education on the Language Development of Spanish-Speaking Children', *Early Childhood Research Quarterly*, **10**, 475–90.

Rogoff, B. *et al.* (1993) 'Toddlers' Guided Participation and their Caregivers in Cultural Activity', in Forman, E., Minick, N. and Stone, C. (Eds) *Contexts for Learning: Sociocultural dynamics in children's development.* New York: Oxford University Press.

SCAA (1996) *Desirable Outcomes for Children's Learning on Entering Compulsory Education.* London: DfEE.

Swain, M. and Cummins, J. (1979) 'Bilingualism, Cognitive Functioning and Education', *Language Teaching and Linguistics Abstracts*, **12** (1), 4–18.

Chapter 4

Continuities and discontinuities: teaching and learning in the home and school of a Puerto Rican five year old

Dinah Volk

The teacher in a bilingual kindergarten reviews the numbers on the calendar with her class.[1]

Teacher:	Let me see. Is Herminio sitting up straight? OK. Let's see. The last number that we did was the number...? What number is this one?
Group:	Ten.
Teacher:	Ten. And who knows what number you count after ten? Nelson?
Nelson:	Eleven.
Teacher:	Eleven. Very good. Eleven has two numbers. What are the two numbers in number eleven?
Group:	One one.

At home Nelson, his parents, older sister, two older brothers, and brother's wife sit around the kitchen table. The adults are talking and Nelson is writing numbers. He asks his mother for help.

Nelson:	Mommy. Ma, how do you make nineteen?
Mother:	A one.
Nelson:	A one and a nine?
Mother:	Mhum. And what comes now after nineteen?
Nelson:	[Still writing] Nineteen. After this one, which one comes next ma?
Mother:	You tell me. Which one comes next?
Nelson:	Twenty.

1 All dialogue in this study was originally in Spanish. It appears here in English translation.

Mother:	How do you write it?
Nelson:	A two and a zero.
Mother:	Mhum.

These exerpts from longer exchanges illustrate the complex web of continuities and discontinuities in language-use patterns between the home of Nelson Maldonado, a Spanish-dominant Puerto Rican five year old, and his bilingual kindergarten classroom. In both exerpts, the adults are conducting lessons. They have identified certain knowledge as important for young children to learn and are using the recitation script, a way of speaking identified with the teacher role. Teacher and mother, Nelson and the other children, all use Spanish, their native language. In the classroom, these lessons are frequent and are dominated by the teacher's questions. Though lessons do occur at home, they are infrequent. In contrast to his classroom behaviour Nelson plays an active role at home, collaborating with his mother to form answers, initiating topics and asking questions.

In this chapter I explore some of these continuities and discontinuities, with a focus on the patterns of questions used by the teacher, parents and children during lessons. The discussion is based on audio recordings, observations and interviews conducted both at home and school over the course of one school year. My purposes in the chapter are (i) to add to a growing body of information on the competencies of children from a variety of cultural backgrounds and their opportunities for learning at home; and (ii) to suggest ways in which teachers can build on these competencies and experiences to help children bridge the gap between home and school. An introduction to some of the research on continuities and discontinuities; the use of questions when listening to children reading; and background information on Nelson's community and school, provide a context for understanding this information.

Continuities and discontinuities

Some researchers (Heath, 1983) argue that the way language is used in families from different cultures and classes and the way it is used in schools is often mutually exclusive and that this discontinuity can help explain why many poor, minority children fail at school. For example, studies of poor African American, Mexican American, and white families suggest that parents provide a rich language environment for children, but rarely, or never, use the 'recitation script'. As a consequence, children's lack of achievement in school is tied first, to their inability to participate in interactions when they are unfamiliar with the way language is used; and second, to teachers' common assumption that this inability reflects resistance, laziness, or lack of content mastery.

Other researchers (Tizard and Hughes, 1984) argue that home–school discontinuities are characterized by varying frequencies in the use of the same kinds of language. When they observed in working-class homes, they saw that elements of the recitation script were used by parents though not as frequently as their children's teachers used them. Children's school failure, according to this position, lies in the inadequacies of their schools and low expectations, not differences in the way language is used.

Still others (Weisner, Gallimore and Jordan, 1993) argue that these generalisations about continuities and discontinuities have led researchers to oversimplify the issue, to focus on differences and ignore similarities, and to create stereotypes by ignoring differences between families from the same culture. The work I discuss here supports this position, suggesting that continuities may coexist with discontinuities in the complex relationship between families and schools.

Questions and teaching

The recitation script, whether used at school or at home, is characterised by familiar questions: known information questions used to assess children's knowledge ('what number comes after nineteen?'); unfinished declaratives used as known information questions ('the last number that we did was the number...?'); questions used as polite, non-explicit directives ('is Herminio sitting up straight?'); questions requesting attention that are used to focus on important information ('remember how we wrote the number 10 yesterday?'). The script is also characterised by the initiation–response–evaluation (IRE) sequence in which the teacher asks for information, the student answers, and the teacher evaluates the answer before moving on.

When using this script, teachers typically ask a string of known information or assessment questions to elicit correct answers, and have children display their knowledge without assistance so that it can be assessed. Children usually answer these questions with words or sentence fragments, trying to provide the desired information. They rarely ask questions about what the teacher means. In contrast, assistance questions prompt children to think in new ways by asking them to elaborate on what they have said and to promote a dialogue with teachers. Despite the fact that teaching needs both assessment *and* assistance questions, the latter are rarely used in schools where teachers concentrate on assessing what children know (Tharp and Gallimore, 1988; Volk, in press).

Nelson: His city and school

Nelson Maldonado lives in a large city in a midwestern state that has had a thriving Puerto Rican community since the late 1940s. In 1990 there were 22,330 Latinos in the city, making up 4.4 per cent of the population. About 90 per cent spoke Spanish at home and the vast majority were Puerto Rican.

In 1991–2, the schools of that city served 71,662 children, 6.5 per cent of whom were Latino. Over 73 per cent came from families living below the poverty level. As a group, the Latino children had both the highest dropout rate and the lowest average reading scores of any in the system. Slightly less than 50 per cent were placed in bilingual classes, making up about 75 per cent of the children in the Bilingual Education Program (de Acosta, 1993).

In Nelson's school, 47 per cent of the children are African American, 22 per cent Latino, and 27 per cent white. Lucia Martin, Nelson's teacher, is a Puerto Rican who was educated in Spanish and English and speaks both fluently. Her morning kindergarten class has 28 children, all native Spanish speakers with varying degrees of English proficiency, and all eligible for the free lunch provided for low-income families.

School activities and the teacher's attitudes and motives

The morning session integrates whole and small group activities, independent work, and play. Learning is active and usually involves interaction with people and materials. Mrs Martin uses Spanish when teaching and slowly introduces English through songs and games. She explains that she believes in expanding children's abilities in Spanish as they learn English and feels it is important to provide positive images of Puerto Rican culture while introducing the children to mainstream American culture. Mrs Martin believes that the children will be successful if she provides an environment in which they are comfortable enough to take risks as they grow in confidence and competence.

Mrs Martin feels that many of the children lack basic experiences and the vocabulary to describe them. Consequently, she feels it is necessary to provide experiences and to help the children connect the experiences with words and articulate them. She organises many activities to facilitate the development of what she calls 'academic language, not just outside experiential language'.

Mrs Martin feels that the children's limitations are caused by their parents' tendency to keep their families safely indoors, and the belief that it is not their place to help their children academically. She feels that even parents like Nelson's, who do provide some experiences and verbal stimulation, need to do more to prepare their children for academic learning. To assist them, she shares materials and ideas for them to use.

Mrs Martin describes Latino children as very dependent on their parents and passive in the classroom. She feels they need to learn to be more independent and curious. Mrs Martin says that, as a Puerto Rican, *she* is struggling to be less authoritarian. With some children who are more verbal, she is learning to step back and let children function more independently. With those with limited experiences and vocabulary, she finds this difficult.

In addition, Mrs Martin feels constrained by the half day class and the pressures from teachers in the next grade to have all children learn a set amount of information. She says she has little time for needed experiences, discussions, and one-to-one interactions with the children.

Nelson and his family: activities, values and motives

Nelson lives with his parents, seven- and 17-year-old brothers, and 14-year-old sister. His 19-year-old brother and his uncle and their wives live nearby. Nelson's father works in a factory; his mother is a housewife. Both parents attended school in Puerto Rico and dropped out at the age of 15, two years before the end of high school.

Nelson's activities at home include playing with action figures, studying his baseball cards, playing draughts, throwing a football, doing jigsaw puzzles, and watching television. He talks, argues, and plays with his older siblings and visiting relatives. Family and friends frequently sit around the kitchen table talking. Nelson sits with them, occasionally joining in, doing homework, colouring, or writing.

Señora Maldonado cleans, cooks and serves food, sews, watches television and talks with family and friends. She makes sure the children do their homework and referees their arguments. When Señor Maldonado comes home, he joins in the talk, watches television, helps with homework and does household repairs.

On one occasion, Nelson's mother reads *Hansel and Gretel* in Spanish to him, asking him to repeat each phrase after her. Then, using a Spanish primer, she helps him read the syllables and words. Nelson's play with his older siblings often has teaching embedded in the activity. For example, Nelson's older brother works with him on a puzzle, sharing strategies for matching pieces. His sister quizzes him on the colours of the draughts game pieces they are using.

Nelson's parents explain that they value education and proudly describe how they are teaching Nelson to write his name, identify colours, numbers and letters, and speak English. Nelson's father asserts that parents bear a responsibility for teaching the basics.

> We don't place all the burden on the teacher. When they go to school they have something and the burden is lighter. That's why we almost never have problems when our children go to school. The teachers say 'I don't have any problem with him because he learns things fast.' But he learns them because we have helped him a lot.

The parents attribute their determination to help their children to their religion. As Jehovah's Witnesses, they help each other and do many activities together, including a weekly series of Bible study sessions. When asked to name the most important thing they can do to help their children in school, Señora Maldonado, reflecting a common Puerto Rican perspective (Lynch and Hanson, 1992), talks about the central role of family togetherness. She asks, 'what good does it do to teach someone maths or teach them to write if the family is not together and there isn't love?'

The Maldonados say they expect their children to do well because they have provided some academic preparation and because they teach their children to respect their teachers. In fact, Nelson did do well in the years after kindergarten, receiving an award in first grade as the best student in his class.

Patterns of language use at home and at school

In the following discussion, I focus on patterns of questioning used by adults and children during lessons, that is, times when the adults provide direct instruction in academic content and skills or discuss relevant experiences. Almost all the talk in both settings is in Spanish. At home, Nelson usually uses English with older siblings. He uses English in school most often with peers during play.

Two patterns of question use at school

In the classroom, Mrs Martin and the children use the recitation script in both large and small group lessons. Questions are used by the teacher, rarely by the children. Of the more than 3,000 questions used during the 21 hours of taping during classroom lessons, only one per cent are asked by all the children in the class. Nelson asks only five questions during that time.

Most of Mrs Martin's questions during lessons assess children's knowledge of important information. She rarely asks them to clarify or elaborate on what they have said. Example 1 below illustrates her use of the recitation script while reviewing the calendar. She uses a series of assessment questions, many requesting known information, to elicit correct answers. The initiation–response–evaluation sequence is also evident. Mrs Martin asks a question – a child responds – Mrs Martin validates the response by repeating it.

Example 1: recitation script at school

Teacher:	Friday. So the last day that we came to school was January eighth and was Friday. What comes after number eight? What number is next? Mónica?
Mónica:	Nine.
Teacher:	And the ninth. The ninth was what day?
Mónica:	Saturday.
Teacher:	Saturday did we come to school?
Group:	No.
Teacher:	No. What number comes after nine? The ...?
Group:	Ten.
Teacher:	The tenth. And the tenth, what day of the week was it? Julio?
Julio:	Sunday.

Mrs Martin is more likely to move away from the recitation script and to ask assistance questions when she is talking to the children about their experiences during lessons. Her intention here is to expand the children's ability to express themselves, to think about what they have said, and to connect their experiences to concepts they are studying. Though Mrs Martin controls the direction of these lessons, the children do talk more and are able to demonstrate their thinking to a greater degree.

In Example 2, during a discussion of the spring weather, Mrs Martin asks open-ended questions ('Nobody did anything good yesterday outside?'); requests elaboration ('When? A long time ago or this weekend?'); and models the use of vocabulary in Spanish ('with swings and slides?' and 'with a basketball?'). The double slashes indicate overlapping speech.

Example 2: open-ended question script at school

Teacher:	Who? Nobody did anything good yesterday outside? Nobody went out to play?...
Teacher:	Mónica, what did you do yesterday?
Mónica:	On, on Saturday I saw a programme called 'Light Clouds' and then when my aunts and my cousin came I went outside to play.
Teacher:	Ah //so you.//
Mónica:	//With my bicycle.//
Teacher:	With your bicycle too. How great. Ofelia what did you do? ...
Teacher:	Mm and did someone someone play in the park with swings and slides? Samuel, did you play like that?
Samuel:	One day I went to the beach.
Teacher:	You went to the beach? When? A long time ago or this weekend? //Yesterday?//
Samuel:	//One day.//
Teacher:	Huh?
Samuel:	[Uses incorrect verb in Spanish]. One day. When, when there wasn't school.
Teacher:	[Models correct verb]. When there wasn't school. And what did you do at the beach?
Samuel:	[Uses incorrect verbs and 'basketball' in English]. I putted a basketball. And playded. And I beat my brother.
Teacher:	You what?
Samuel:	I pu-putted a basketball hoop.
Teacher:	[Uses 'basketball' in English, then Spanish]. Oh you played with a basketball. With a basketball? Who else played outside yesterday? Tell me.

The children's use of questions during lessons is different from the teacher's. They never ask known information questions but are more likely to ask unknown information questions to which they do not have the answer ('how do you do it?'); to ask for permission ('can I do this?'); to ask for clarification ('on the left side?'); and to ask for confirmation ('all of this, right?'). These differences reflect the children's awareness that they are supposed to focus on what the teacher is saying during lessons rather than on what they are saying or thinking.

Question use at home

In Nelson's home we find one 35 minute formal lesson during the 11 hours of taping as well as many pieces of adult instruction, some short and some longer, that are embedded in other activities. Interestingly, the parents use aspects of the recitation script during these times. Example 3 contains exerpts from a lesson Señora Maldonado conducts with a Spanish primer bought in Puerto Rico when her daughter was learning to read. She uses the traditional approach to teaching reading in Spanish, introducing simple syllables and combining them into words. Like the teacher, she uses known information questions to assess Nelson's knowledge ('how do you say M I?'); polite, non-explicit directives ('how would you say it?'); and unfinished declaratives ('A?'). The IRE sequence is used repeatedly. Nelson's brother, Robert, helps out at first.

Example 3: recitation script at home

Mother:	Mhum. And this one?
Robert:	[Whispers] Map.
Nelson:	Pi...pe.
Mother:	And this one?
Nelson:	Poppa?
Mother:	Mhum.
Nelson:	Pu? Let me see. Pu. Yes.
Mother:	No, that one isn't there.
Nelson:	Ma. No.
Mother:	Yes. How would you say it?
Nelson:	Ma.
Mother:	How would you say it?
Nelson:	The same as this one?
Mother:	Mhum. Aha.
Nelson:	Puma.
Mother:	Puma.
Nelson:	//Here.//
Mother:	//Here.// So here in this one.
Nelson:	Oh. A...dd. Add?
Mother:	Mhum.

Nelson:	To add?
Mother:	Mhum. What are you going to add? What do you add?
Nelson:	Ah.
Mother:	Nu.
Nelson:	Numbers.
Mother:	You add numbers.
Nelson:	Up to here?
Mother:	'M I' How do you say 'M I'?
Nelson:	Mi. Ma.
Mother:	That one? Ss.
Nelson:	So.
Mother:	Ss. Remember. What's this? A what? A?
Nelson:	Sa.
Mother:	Aha...

This is the only pattern of questioning that the parents use in lessons. They model their teaching on the traditional recitation script that they have experienced and that they have seen their children's teachers use. Like the teacher, they ask many assessment questions and ask the children to clarify what they have said much less than they do ordinarily.

Nonetheless, the lesson script at home is not an exact replica of the lesson script in school. The parents lead the lessons but collaborate with Nelson along the way. He participates actively by initiating topics, helping to decide what and how much to do, and by talking almost as frequently as they do and by asking the same amount and kinds of questions. Of the 114 questions asked during home lessons, 53 per cent are asked by Nelson, 46 per cent by his parents, and 1 per cent by siblings. As in the excerpts that open this chapter and in Example 3, Nelson often asks for clarification ('the same as this one?'); or confirmation ('a one and a nine?' and 'poppa?') of what the parent has said. He gives partial answers which work together with the information provided by his parent to produce more complete answers, as in the sequence of questions about adding in Example 3.

Summary and implications for practice

Table 4.1 illustrates the complex web of continuities and discontinuities in language-use patterns between Nelson's home and school. In this section I discuss some of these relationships and offer suggestions for Mrs Martin to extend her practice of building on Nelson's competencies and experiences and to help parents learn from her.

Table 4.1 Continuities[1] and discontinuities in lessons in school and at home

Lesson Components	School	Home
personnel	*children with adult* large/small groups	*child with adult* one-to-one, others present
cultural values	*education important* *maintenance of L1 and culture* children unprepared adult as authority, children empowered	*education important* *maintenance of L1 and culture* child prepared child respects adult
task	*use of Spanish* relevant experiences and *academic content* teacher initiated and centred	*use of Spanish* *academic content* *parent initiated,* collaborative
immediate motives	*to teach knowledge and skills* to provide concrete experiences to develop language and thinking *to prepare children for next grade*	*to teach knowledge and skills* *to prepare child for school*
script	*recitation script* and open-ended questioning teacher asks questions, children answer *teacher requests known information* children request *clarification* rarely	*recitation script* parent and child ask and answer questions *parent requests known information* child requests *clarification* often

1 Continuities are in italic for emphasis and clarification.

Overall, it is clear that both the teacher and parents create continuity for Nelson by mutually supporting each other. Mrs Martin relates to the children as a Puerto Rican and native Spanish speaker, promoting their language development and learning in Spanish. She urges the parents to work with her and sends home materials for teaching more formally. She encourages children to talk about their experiences and communicates her expectation that they can succeed.

The Maldonados attend conferences and meetings, check Nelson's homework, teach him to respect teachers, expect he will do well in school, and teach him necessary academic skills and information using the recitation script, a pattern of questioning they know is valued in school. These efforts create learning experiences with strong links between expectations and language use, establishing continuity between home and school. Though Nelson's parents may not be representative of all Puerto Rican parents – any more than Mrs Martin represents all teachers – they certainly represent some Puerto Rican parents who see themselves as active agents in their children's learning.

Most often, discussions of home-school relationships are based on the assumption that such continuity is better for children than discontinuity. In this case, however, an important aspect of the continuity is the use of the recitation script that is described almost universally as constraining children's language and learning. While the use of this script at home probably does facilitate Nelson's learning in school, merely matching this script in both settings may not, in the long run, benefit him.

For teachers, this suggests the importance of understanding and valuing patterns of teaching and learning in homes, and building on these patterns as they draw children into the world of schooling and academic inquiry (Tharp and Gallimore, 1988). Thus, Mrs Martin might use assessment questions, and slowly and explicitly introduce children to more challenging assistance questions when discussing academic content, not just personal experiences. In this way she could scaffold the children's understanding and participation as they learn to use language and think in new ways. When teaching reading, she might use the traditional Spanish method of combining syllables that is used by Nelson's mother, while introducing the practice of reading and writing rooted in one's own experiences and language. Stories sent home and read and repeated word for word could be read again and discussed in school (Gregory, 1996).

As shown in Table 4.1, there are also a number of discontinuities between lessons at home and in school. Two important and related discontinuities stand out. First, the teacher believes that many of the children, including Nelson, are not prepared by their parents for kindergarten. This belief affects her attitudes and the constraining language she uses. The parents have a different perspective. It is their job to prepare Nelson, not to formally teach him as a teacher would, and they feel that they have done so.

This suggests the importance of Mrs Martin acknowledging and appreciating the parents' efforts, and the concern and values that support these efforts. Once a positive relationship is established, Mrs Martin can work with parents to identify the many interactions and materials in the homes that facilitate children's learning, and to suggest new ones that build on parents' knowledge and strengths.

The critical role played by older siblings in teaching Nelson through play could also be acknowledged. Along with the parents, Mrs Martin might explore ways of encouraging their interactions, integrating older siblings into homework and even asking them to help in the classroom. Inviting children from older classes into the kindergarten to work with the students would be another way for Mrs Martin to build on children's learning experiences at home.

The second important discontinuity relates to beliefs about the relative power of adults and children. Mrs Martin believes that teachers should maintain their authority but that children should be empowered to make choices and be active. The language she uses is inconsistent with these values though it is consistent with her belief that many of the children are ill-prepared for school.

The parents, for their part, believe that teaching their children to respect the teacher and be quiet and deferential is part of their preparation for school. Though this belief is not consistent with Mrs Martin's emphasis on active children, it is consistent with the parents' motives and cultural values. Ironically, the children are more active in lessons with their parents than they are in lessons with the teacher.

This suggests that Mrs Martin could teach in ways more consistent with her own beliefs by encouraging the children's questions and active participation, listening more to what they have to say, and asking them to clarify and elaborate on their answers – not just assessing them (Morgan and Sexton, 1991; Wells, 1993). Lessons that integrate academic content with more open-ended and responsive questioning might result in higher levels of participation and competence for the children, helping to persuade Mrs Martin that they are more prepared than she thinks.

Finally, it is important to recognise the need for school-wide support for Mrs Martin's desire to provide more experiential learning and one-to-one interactions. A full-day class and agreements among teachers in different grades to focus on expanding children's competencies, not just filling them with information and assessing it, would support her efforts to change.

Conclusion

Much of the previous work comparing teaching and learning in homes and schools has emphasised continuities *or* discontinuities as if they were mutually exclusive. Such work usually shares suggestions for recreating home interaction patterns in school or, more commonly, training parents to recreate school interaction patterns at home. Nelson's story illustrates a more complex and dynamic process. While problematic discontinuities certainly exist for children from cultures different than the culture of their schools, varying degrees of continuity may also exist for many of those children. In addition, some discontinuities may lead teachers, parents, and children in new and productive directions as they actively affect each other's practice.

The use of the recitation script by Nelson's parents, though infrequent, is significant because it suggests that parents do not just use one style of teaching linked to their culture. They are influenced by what occurs in school and may incorporate into their teaching language and techniques that they perceive to be valued there. School becomes one of several sources, including cultural heritage, that influence how parents talk and interact with their children (Vasquez, Pease-Alvarez, and Shannon, 1994).

As professionals, teachers must develop ways to learn about, and understand, children's cultures and the language of learning in their homes. They must work jointly with parents and children – teaching them and learning from them – to combine styles of everyday language use with language styles used for learning and inquiry at home and in school.

Acknowledgements

This research was supported in part by The Faculty Associate Program of the Urban Child Research Center, College of Urban Affairs, Cleveland State University, Cleveland, Ohio.

References

de Acosta, M. (1993) *The Cleveland Hispanic Community and Education: A struggle for voice.* Cleveland, Ohio: Urban Child Research Center, Cleveland State University.

Gregory, E. (1996) *Making Sense of a New World: Learning to read in a second language.* London: Paul Chapman.

Heath, S.B. (1983) *Ways with Words: Language, life, and work in communities and classrooms.* Cambridge: Cambridge University Press.

Lynch, E.W. and Hanson, M.J. (1992) *Developing Cross-Cultural Competence: A guide for working with young children and their families.* Baltimore, Maryland: Paul H. Brookes.

Morgan, N. and Sexton, J. (1991) *Teaching, Questioning, and Learning.* London: Routledge.

Tharp, R.G. and Gallimore, R. (1988) *Rousing Minds to Life: Teaching, learning, and schooling in a social context.* Cambridge: Cambridge University Press.

Tizard, B. and Hughes, M. (1984) *Young Children Learning.* Cambridge, Mass: Harvard University Press.

Vasquez, O.A., Pease-Alvarez, L. and Shannon, S.M. (1994) *Pushing Boundaries: Language and culture in a Mexicano community.* Cambridge: Cambridge University Press.

Volk, D. (in press) 'Questions in lessons: Activity settings in the homes and school of two Puerto Rican kindergartners', *Anthropology and Education Quarterly.*

Weisner, T.S., Gallimore, R. and Jordan, C. (1993) 'Unpackaging cultural effects of classroom learning: Hawaiian peer assistance and child-generated activity'. in R.N. Roberts (Ed.) *Coming Home to Preschool: The sociocultural context of early education* (pp. 59–87). Norwood, NJ: Ablex.

Wells, G. (1993) 'Re-evaluating the IRE sequence', *Linguistics and Education, 5,* 1–37.

Chapter 5

Stories from two worlds: bilingual experiences between fact and fiction

Michaela Ulich and Pamela Oberhuemer

Zeynep is four years old and lives with her parents and baby sister in a block of flats close to the main station in Munich. Her father and mother, Erdal and Ayla, are both Turkish. Erdal was born in Munich and is one of the so-called second-generation migrants whose fathers came to Germany during the early 1970s. He works – as his father did for over 20 years – for the large automobile company BMW. Ayla grew up in Turkey and came to Germany as a 15 year old ten years ago.

Ayla, Zeynep's mother, speaks a few rudimentary words of German. At home she speaks Turkish. Erdal, Zeynep's father, who is quite fluent in German, prefers to communicate in Turkish at home, not only with his wife but also with his children. On weekdays, Zeynep spends about six hours a day with her grandparents, mostly with her grandmother, who speaks no German at all. So for Zeynep, Turkish is very definitely her 'home' language. Although there are, of course, exceptions, this is the language situation of many children whose family culture is significantly different from the dominant culture.

Starting kindergarten – what will it bring?

In September Zeynep will be starting kindergarten. Her parents – and grandparents – generally feel this is a good idea. They say 'It's time she started learning some of the things she will need in school', and 'It will be good for her German'.

At the same time there are apprehensions. Her grandmother has heard that it is a Catholic-run kindergarten. Will Zeynep be expected to take part in Christian acts of worship? Will she hear a lot of New Testament stories? Her mother has not yet been into the kindergarten (Erdal took care of the registration), but she has heard from a friend that the children change clothes for physical activities. Do boys and girls get undressed in the same room? Zeynep's father is sceptical about the young teacher in her early twenties who will be in charge of Zeynep's group. Can she possibly manage a group on her own? Even the female kindergarten director seems to be no older than himself.

German parents will almost certainly not share these particular apprehensions (although they may have others). After all, they have easy access to cultural knowledge, transmitted over the generations, about kindergartens and kindergarten rituals in Germany. But Zeynep's parents and grandparents do not. The reservations they may have are not issues they will discuss with Zeynep, but they are issues which will affect their behaviour. And Zeynep will notice these apprehensions, even though they are not explicitly expressed. She will notice that her mother cannot talk to her group teacher as the other mothers do; she will notice the way her father communicates with the kindergarten director – and maybe feel embarrassed; she will notice that her grandmother disapproves when she talks about a visit to the local church. She will be experiencing institutionalised culture for the first time, and she will notice that 'her' language and 'her' culture are not part of the 'kindergarten culture'. Maybe in the end she will prefer not to talk about the kindergarten at home, or to talk about home in the kindergarten.

How many Turkish children in Germany experience this kind of ambivalence at an early age, and how do they cope with the conflicting feelings that arise out of situations like these? We do not know exactly. But we do know that a lack of self-esteem – of cultural self-esteem – is prohibitive when it comes to getting to grips with the world, to constructing knowledge and testing learning through language or, in the case of Zeynep, through two languages.

How can we help children negotiate these transitions? The need to seek answers to this question becomes all the more pressing as migration, and with it the number of children experiencing the consequences of migration, increases worldwide. Before we focus more closely on the kinds of expectations and assumptions which may hinder Zeynep in her transition 'between two worlds', and suggest ways of helping to support her emergent bilingual and bicultural identity, let us first take a look at the changing composition and size of the non-German population in Germany.

Who are the 'foreigners'?

Germany has a population of 81.6 million. Persons classified as 'foreigners' (*Ausländer*) are those with a passport from a country other than Germany. Today they represent 8.6 per cent of the total population, the majority residing in former West Germany. Approximately one per cent live in the eastern federal states (Beauftragte der Bundesregierung, 1995). Since the early 1970s, between 10 and 15 per cent of all children born in Germany come from a non-German family (12.9 per cent in 1993).

However, it is becoming more and more difficult – both statistically and culturally – to differentiate between the German and the non-German population. There are a number of reasons for this.

* One quarter of the minority population has been living in the country for more than 20 years, and almost 60 per cent for 10 or more years.
* Two-thirds of all children from non-German family backgrounds are born in Germany.
* The number of marriages between Germans and members of the migrant population has increased considerably (from roughly 28,000 in 1980 to about 39,800 in 1990).

Despite this, Germany still does not consider itself officially to be an 'immigration country' (*Einwanderungsland*). Members of the non-German population are generally referred to as 'foreigners' or 'migrants', and not as 'immigrants'. Apart from the European Union member state nationals, who may now vote at local elections, the foreign population as a whole has no voting rights at any political level. The amount of so-called 'structural discrimination' is still considerable – whether in the search for employment, for accommodation, or in schools (Bommes and Radtke, 1993).

Families from Turkey form by far the largest group, accounting for just over 28 per cent of the foreign cultural community at the end of 1994. A quarter of the foreign population are members of the European Union – predominantly from Italy, Greece, Austria, Spain, Portugal, the Netherlands and Britain. Following the radical political changes in Europe at the end of the 1980s, there was an upsurge of east-west migration to Germany between 1988 and 1992. During this period total numbers of the foreign population rose from four and a half million to six and a half million. In particular, large numbers of ethnic German families from Poland, Romania and the former Soviet Union migrated to Germany. At the same time the number of political refugees and asylum-seekers rose steadily up to mid-1993, when more restrictive practices were introduced by the German government. In 1992 more than one and a half million refugees were registered in Germany, many of them victims of the war in former Yugoslavia.

This means that in German kindergartens and schools there are:

• Children of second- and third-generation migrant worker families, mostly from Turkey and from southern European countries.

• Children of ethnic German origin from eastern European countries and the former Soviet Union who often speak little or no German on arrival.

• Children of asylum seekers and political refugees, mostly from former Yugoslavia, and from African and Asian countries.

The percentage of migrant children attending kindergartens is significantly lower than that of German children (approximately 58 per cent compared with 74 per cent in 1992). At the same time, in some kindergartens in inner city areas there are kindergarten groups in which over half the children come from non-German family backgrounds. Working with children and parents from diverse backgrounds has thus become a common feature of professional practice for many early childhood practitioners.

Cultural assumptions and expectations

What is often underestimated – or sometimes completely overlooked – when working in groups with a mixed cultural intake is the fact that families from other cultural backgrounds often have expectations which may differ considerably from the mainstream patterns of many professionals (*see* Gregory, 1994 for an account of the differing cultural assumptions between Bangladeshi families and British teachers in early years classrooms).

Between home and kindergarten Zeynep will be met by a number of expectations and aspirations concerning her stay in kindergarten, her development, her schooling, and her future. These implicit and explicit values will, of course, be manifold and depend on the family's social status and migration history, and on the parents' individual educational and cultural background. We will not attempt to cover inter-group variations and individual differences. Our purpose here is to focus on selected culture-based assumptions and educational expectations. We shall be constructing and delineating types of expectations, we shall not be describing a real-life scenario with all its complexities and ambivalences. We have selected both parental and professional expectations, which tend to draw a dividing line between home and school, between different languages and cultures. We are discussing this particular set of assumptions and excluding others, because the teacher's assumptions and beliefs about Zeynep's home language and culture will make it harder for Zeynep to cope with the transition from home to school and to develop a positive, truly bilingual and bicultural identity.

The family's cultural and linguistic background: problems of status

Examining practitioners' images and expectations concerning Turkish and Muslim culture means relating educational settings to the wider dominant political culture. In this eurocentric culture, Turkish as a language has no public presence or prestige: it is neither a generally accepted and high-status language like English or French, nor is it automatically considered an asset to be able to speak both Turkish and German. Turkish is the language of the 'family', of the private sphere, it may be important for the child in relation to some past or future ties to the home country, but not in relation the child's identity here and now in Germany.

Eurocentric stereotypes about Muslim culture are well known and need only be touched upon:
- 'There is a wide gap between Middle European and Turkish Muslim culture.'
- 'Women and girls are oppressed.'
- 'Men have the say.'
- 'Traditional sex role models cause problems for Turkish girls and women.'
- 'Most Turkish families are conservative in outlook.'

Needless to say these are not merely stereotypes – they can be very real problems as well. The question in our case is not whether these stereotypes are true or false, or whether they are based on fact or fiction. Our purpose is to identify a few standard assumptions Zeynep may be met with on entering kindergarten; they will belong to Zeynep's social world as constructed by adults, no matter whether they are justified or not.

What about the parents? The more traditional Turkish families sending their child to kindergarten may see a world of difference between Christian and Muslim culture. They will be worried that, by attending a German kindergarten, their child will be estranged from Muslim culture and norms – especially customs concerning religious practices (food, religious festivals, etc), kinship ties, respect for adults and elders, sexual mores and sex roles. At this level there is fear of assimilation.

What is a child supposed to 'learn' in kindergarten?

Turkish parents tend to view kindergarten both as an institution where parents may leave their children to be taken care of while they are at work, and as a place where children 'learn' something. The question is: 'what is the child supposed to learn?' 'Learning for life' – as German pedagogues phrase it – as opposed to schooling and formal instruction, is something that in Turkish culture is traditionally associated with family and kinship ties, with non-institutionalised everyday life and local social networks. The idea of kindergarten as an 'holistic' environment, as a chance to communicate and negotiate with peers and develop social competence, as a chance to learn through play, is not familiar to Turkish parents. Rather, institutions with teachers are meant to instruct children, to teach them skills that will be useful in school. This is not an attitude unique to Turkish parents. Kindergarten educators report that German parents – especially those with five-year-old children who are to start school the following year – also tend to be increasingly concerned about what their children are actually 'learning' in kindergarten in preparation for school.

Now for Turkish parents this concern about their child's future in the educational system is of course more poignant. It is directly and painfully related to a child's German language competence. Kindergarten is, among other things, a ticket that is being bought in advance to give the child a chance in mainstream German education. Thus, once in kindergarten, the child should learn German as quickly as possible.

'She must learn German – as quickly as possible'

Parents tend to look upon learning German as a unique and distinct process which must have priority over all others. Turkish language competence is not immediately related to this process, there is no holistic view of the child's language development. At this level, a desire for the child's speedy assimilation seems to be the parents' guiding principle.

Teachers will hear parents asking: 'How is she getting on in German?' 'Is she really learning German, or is she just playing around most of the time?' They will not only feel pressured by parental demands; they will have experienced again and again that fluency in the German language is looked upon by school teachers as a crucial factor in academic achievement, or even as a pre-requisite for admittance to mainstream schooling. Generally speaking, German teachers have received no special training on characteristics of bilingualism and second-language acquisition; this is not part of the standard curriculum in pre-service training.

The whole situation can be frustrating and stressful for the kindergarten teacher. She may feel that she should be 'teaching' Zeynep to speak better German. She may not have the professional knowledge and the self-confidence to tell parents (as well as herself) that, especially at the age of four, Zeynep will learn most during play or through informal, pleasurable conversation with adults and peers. Worrying about Zeynep's German language competence may mean that she starts focusing on language as such. This in turn could lead to a series of language-related attitudes and educational measures which may deeply affect Zeynep's motivation to express herself and communicate, both in German and in Turkish.

Monolingual perceptions of bilinguals

As a rule, language competence is not measured for a child's overall language repertoire, it is assessed only for one language and with reference to monolingual standards in that language. Moreover, it is often assumed that one language can only improve at the expense of the other. All these assumptions are part of a 'monolingual' view of bilingualism (Grosjean, 1985 and Baker, 1996).

This monolingual view often contends that bilinguals will have problems in cognitive processing as a result of the potential muddle between two insufficiently-developed languages. A common assumption is that children who are exposed to two languages risk semi-lingualism. Although more than one half of the world's population grows up with two or more languages, this is not part of German 'linguistic culture'. A child exposed to, and living in, two or more languages is still seen as something unusual. Several assumptions follow from this:

• Only the very best children will learn German properly.
• Speaking Turkish is an obstacle on the way to becoming fluent in German.
• Children who grow up with two languages need special training and instruction in order to learn one language (namely German) properly.

Focusing on language

Since emergent bilinguals are judged to be at risk of semi-lingualism it is assumed that special attention must be paid to their language performance. This may lead to the following measures and attitudes in educational settings.

• Zeynep is singled out for sessions of formal teaching and language instruction.
• When Zeynep speaks German the teacher is especially sensitive to mistakes in grammar and feels that Zeynep should be corrected (directly or indirectly).
• When Zeynep addresses other children or the teacher, less attention will be paid to *what* she is trying to say, to her message, and more importance will be given to *how* she is saying it, how well or how poorly she is expressing herself. She will be praised – or corrected – accordingly.
• The teacher will make an effort to improve and extend Zeynep's vocabulary; this may mean teaching specific words and creating situations which for Zeynep will feel more like an oral vocabulary test than like a normal conversation.

All this may have short-term effects in improving language competence; it will not, in the long run, make Zeynep feel at ease with German. Above all, it will not enhance her imagination and motivation.

Living with two languages

Adults worrying about Zeynep learning German may tend to forget that she is actually living with two languages. We deliberately say *living with* two languages, rather than *speaking* two languages. It seems very important to shift attention away from bilingualism as a question of language proficiency that can be assessed, to bilingualism as way of life, as something that is being lived and experienced by the child. Grosjean (1982) expressed this change of perspective in the title of his book *Life with Two Languages*. This entails developing a truly holistic view of bilingualism, accepting two languages as part of a child's life and development, with all its consequences (Grosjean, 1985).

An holistic view suggests that bilinguals should not be seen as people composed of two separate parts. The bilingual is not two monolinguals in one person but a unity different from a monolingual – with a specific linguistic and cultural profile. This approach looks upon a child's development as an ongoing process of 'biculturation' and of language acquisition encompassing first *and* second languages.

We have dwelt on this point because, besides being an issue in research and literature on bilingualism, it also touches upon a more elementary level concerning Zeynep's life at home and in kindergarten. It helps us to take her perspective and actually accept her living with two cultures and languages; thus we may give her a chance to integrate two languages and different cultures, thereby creating something new.

So far we have discussed implicit theories and attitudinal patterns. All of them dealt with the relationship between two cultures and two languages, as well as the status of a minority language and culture within mainstream educational settings. Now we will leap from theory to practice.

What can be done to make the presence of various cultures and languages in kindergarten a concrete and pleasurable experience for minority and majority children? One procedure is to introduce ethnic stories and language events which will be rewarding and self-enhancing for both minority and majority children.

The public and the private sphere

A teacher introducing a Turkish-German audio-cassette, or a Turkish picture book, is offering a fairly neutral and non-threatening platform for intercultural exchange – unlike the more personal and individual request addressed to immigrant children to talk about their families. Many immigrant children want to be like all the 'others', and in this situation the well-meaning request 'now tell us about your grandmother in Turkey' may be met with silence. In comparison, books, songs, films or fairytales are forms of public cultural expression, which can be either readily accepted or overlooked by the child – depending on the situation and his/her frame of mind. A story or a film is basically open to many different reactions which need not be immediately related to a child's individual situation. A child may, indeed, use a Turkish picture book to introduce his Turkish grandmother, but he can do so by choice, at his own pace. There is no pressure to talk about Turkey or Turkish customs, one may talk about the story simply as a 'good' or a 'boring' story. An active and flexible presentation of children's literature from different countries may lead to a series of follow-up activities which need not be restricted to the immigrant community. They may involve German families, as well as different nationalities. Organising a series of shadow theatre performances from different countries may perhaps transcend the food and folklore fraternisations on special occasions.

Experiments in dual language presentation through intercultural films and videos

The idea of the series *medien interKulturell* (Ulich and Oberhuemer, 1991, 1992) was to develop imaginative and pleasurable dual language presentations for mixed audiences (including monolingual German children) by integrating foreign language elements into a run-on story or into a game playing on children's curiosity and imagination. This idea is based on an approach developed by Erman Okay, a Turkish writer of children's plays in Germany. Various techniques were developed: two languages within a fairy-tale atmosphere, a slapstick dramatisation of communication problems and a live presentation of children exchanging childlore from different countries. The Turkish-German audio-cassette *Keloglan and the Giant* exemplifies this approach.

This story was adapted from the original by a Turkish immigrant in Germany. It has become a blend of traditional and modern elements. Keloglan is so well-known as a folk hero that most Turkish families can relate to him, regardless of their background. At the same time, Okay's adaptation is an original contribution to modern children's literature. In his version Keloglan, the little man who makes his way in the world, is self-assertive towards the Padishah. In the end, he refuses to accept the Padishah's daughter as a gift. Instead he chooses to marry the bright girl who helps him outwit the giant.

The title story of the cassette (Okay, 1991) features Keloglan in his trials against the fearful giant in the Kaf mountains. A narrator's voice announces that this tale originally came from Anatolia and that he will tell the story in German and in Turkish. There is no translation, but rather a dramatic give-and-take between two languages. For the most part the dialogue is such that German-speaking children can infer from the (German) answer what is being said in Turkish – the plot and acoustic effects also help.

This dual language presentation is not realistically motivated (unlike plays where the boss speaks in German, the workers or maids in Turkish). In this case, switching between languages is part of the whole make-believe atmosphere of a fairy tale and it comes as naturally as Keloglan flying or being turned into a horse or a flower. In view of the German-speaking mixed audiences we are trying to reach, the dominant language is German, i.e. the narrative voice is German. Yet both languages are, dramatically speaking, equal. They are both essential to the plot. This presentation of Turkish and German on an equal level symbolises the parity of a dominant and of a minority language and it dramatises a familiar situation for bilingual minority children: permanent switching between two languages. Even younger German children and other children who do not speak Turkish greatly enjoy the presentation – in both kindergarten and school. They enjoy following the story and become curious to know what is being said and often hedge a guess. There is no frustration or impatience at 'not understanding' as they experience a foreign language in a make-believe situation full of suspense. Turkish-speaking children enjoy hearing Turkish in a German-speaking context; and they can play on their bilingual competencies and use them in a group situation with German children and not only in an ethnically homogeneous group. Both German-speaking and Turkish-speaking children witness the acceptance and valuing of a Turkish tale and of Turkish as a language within a mainstream educational and cultural setting, within the institution. In *Keloglan and the Giant* the two languages belong to an organic whole; after a while, once the story gets going, the audience tends to forget which language is being used.

Stories – a starting point for intercultural dialogue

Our approach focuses on:
- Fostering positive attitudes and matter-of-fact interplay between different cultures.
- Enhancing German children's and families' awareness of other cultures and languages in a mainstream setting.
- Helping to meet the needs of emergent bilinguals, strengthening their bicultural identity, and offering them opportunities to demonstrate their specific skills within an institutional setting in the dominant cultural context.

In our work we chose to focus on stories – a common element both of childlore and educational activities across cultures – as a starting point for intercultural dialogue: as a vehicle for creating common ground in culturally mixed groups, and as a way of establishing a sense of uncomplicated, everyday inclusion and acceptance of different cultures and languages among children, parents and educators.

References

Baker, C. (1996) 'Perceptions of Bilinguals', *European Journal of Intercultural Studies*, **7** (1), 45–50.

Beauftragte der Bundesregierung für die Belange der Ausländer (1995). Bericht über die Lage der Ausländer in der Bundesrepublik Deutschland. Bonn.

Bommes, M. and Radtke, F. O. (1993) 'Institutionalisierte Diskriminierung von Migrantenkindern; die Herstellung ethnischer Differenz in der Schule', *Zeitschrift für Pädagogik*, **39**, 483-497.

Gregory, E. (1994) 'Cultural Assumptions and Early Years' Pedagogy: The effect of the home culture on minority children's interpretation of reading in school', *Language, Culture and Curriculum*, **7** (2), 1–14.

Grosjean, F. (1982) *Life with Two Languages. An introduction to bilingualism.* Cambridge, Mass: Harvard University Press.

Grosjean, F. (1985) 'The bilingual as a competent but specific speaker-hearer', *Journal of Multilingual and Multicultural Development*, **6** (6), 467–77.

Okay, E. (1991) *Keloglan und der Riese*. Märchen in deutscher und türkischer Sprache. Mit Begleitheft von P. Oberhuemer and M. Ulich: Zwischen Keloglan und Rotkäppchen. Weinheim und Basel: Beltz 1991.

Ulich, M., and Oberhuemer, P. (Eds) (1985, 3rd revised edition, 1993). Es war einmal, es war keinmal... Ein multikulturelles Lese- und Arbeitsbuch. Weinheim, Basel: Beltz. (*Anthology of children's literature from Turkey, former Yugoslavia, Greece, Italy, Spain and Portugal, with supplementary texts for teachers*)

Ulich, M., Oberhuemer, P. and Reidelhuber, A. (Eds) (1987, 5th revised edition, 1995). Der Fuchs geht um... auch anderswo. Ein multikulturelles Spiel- und Arbeitsbuch. Weinheim und Basel: Beltz. (*Anthology of games, rhymes, songs, festive days and customs, etc. from Turkey, former Yugoslavia, Greece, Italy, Spain and Portugal, with supplementary texts for teachers*)

Ulich, M. and Oberhuemer, P. (Eds) (1991, 1992): medien interKulturell. 4 Tonkassetten mit Begleitheften. Weinheim und Basel: Beltz. (*A series of four video-cassettes and four audio-cassettes, each accompanied by a supplementary booklet of about 60-80 pages providing relevant background information, texts in the minority language, and suggestions for practical work. The cassettes present Turkish and Italian fairytales and stories, literary folk heroes, traditional and modern games alongside children's literature and folk culture from Germany.*)

Chapter 6

A child writes from her everyday world: using home texts to develop biliteracy at school

Charmian Kenner

'I want my Gujarati'. 'I want to write like my mum.' These statements were made by Meera at the age of four, when her mother came into her south London nursery class to write in the family's home language. As well as showing a strong positive response to her mother's presence as a writer in the nursery, Meera displayed considerable interest in literacy materials, which were part of her cultural background, brought in from home. She made use of these as a base from which to develop her own writing in Gujarati and in English.

As a researcher working with the class teacher to investigate young children's knowledge about home literacies, I was able to observe and interact with Meera in the classroom over the course of a whole school year. In this case study I shall discuss how the opportunity to work with home texts in school aided Meera's literacy development in both languages.

Background

There is evidence that as young children participate in everyday events involving written language, they come to understand how particular texts are used within particular patterns of social interaction. Taylor (1983) gives examples such as children writing messages and get well cards for family members, and making signs to advertise a lemonade stall as part of imaginative play. Harste, Woodward and Burke (1984) show that five year olds can produce recognisable versions of letters and maps, whilst Bissex (1980) describes her six-year-old son's 'newspapers', containing sections for weather, news, cartoons and advertisements. Such examples demonstrate children's awareness of the content and symbols appropriate to each type of text.

Children can gain a wealth of information about literacy from a variety of home backgrounds, as shown by Taylor and Dorsey-Gaines' study of inner-city families in the United States (1988). Patterns of interaction around text, however, tend to differ between communities (Heath, 1983). A range of literacy practices within multilingual contexts in Britain has been documented by Saxena (1994) and Bhatt and Martin-Jones (1997) from research with Panjabi families in Southall and Gujarati families in Leicester. In these communities, children participate in the uses of home language texts for cultural and religious reasons, and to keep in touch with relatives elsewhere. Reading and writing takes place in a variety of scripts, depending on the purpose of each text.

The project described here aimed to discover what kinds of understandings three and four year olds were bringing from their home literacy experiences to school. As well as looking at literacy knowledge in English, we were interested to find out whether bilingual children at this age recognised that writing in their home languages was used in specific practices within their families and communities, and whether they already had some knowledge about the visual appearance of different types of script. Our educational concern was to enable children to build on these understandings in their literacy learning at school.

Together, the nursery teacher and I set out to construct a school environment which would connect with children's home literacy experiences. The roleplay area ('home corner') was already a site where children could act out a variety of situations with the help of props such as household furniture and cooking utensils. We made sure that a constant supply of everyday literacy materials was also provided in this area: calendars, telephone directories, magazines, catalogues, writing paper, envelopes, notepads and pens. We found that children made frequent use of these in their roleplay.

Bilingual parents helped us by bringing in materials which they used in their first language at home; these included newspapers, calendars, alphabet teaching aids, and a variety of videos. We also asked parents to write in their home languages for particular purposes in the nursery. The school was situated in Brixton, a multiracial area in south London, and children's linguistic and cultural backgrounds were enormously varied. Languages used at home included Yoruba, Spanish, Gujarati, Thai, Arabic, Tigrinya, Pilipino and Cantonese. Materials in all these languages were made available by parents to the nursery, and children made many written responses as a result.

As parents became involved in the project, I arranged informal interviews with them at the nursery, to find out more about children's home experiences of literacy events in English and in other languages. This information, along with observations and tapescripts of children's interactions as they engaged in writing in the nursery, and the texts which resulted, made it possible to build up a picture of what children knew about literacy and how their writing developed over the course of that school year.

Meera was a constant presence in activities taking place in the home corner and the writing area. The texts she produced, and her comments about them, gave a particularly clear indication of the connections which can be forged between literacy at home and at school. I shall now look at these connections in detail.

Meera and her family

Meera was three years ten months old when the project began, and four years eight months by the end of the school year. Her immediate family consisted of herself, her nine-year-old sister Pinal, and her mother and father. Meera's grandparents lived in Gujarat, in north-west India, where her parents had lived before coming to England. Pinal and Meera had been born and brought up in London; the family ran a small local supermarket not far from the school.

At home, Meera's parents spoke to each other, and mainly to the children, in Gujarati, whilst Pinal, as the older sister who had entered the British school system first, played with Meera in English as well as in Gujarati. Meera's mother read Gujarati newspapers and used Gujarati to write letters to relatives in India; Meera's father wrote in English only.

Meera thus had a rich variety of literacy experiences, at home and in her family's shop, in both Gujarati and English. In this chapter, I shall consider the following aspects of her literacy development: how she related to the world of the shop in home corner play at school, how she related to school literacy at home, how she reacted to texts which were part of Gujarati family culture when these were used at school; and how her writing development showed an interaction between English and Gujarati. In each of these areas, family relationships, particularly Meera's relationship with her sister, played a key part in structuring her literacy development.

Relating to shop literacy at school

Meera's sense of pride in her family's shop was emphasised when the nursery children stopped outside it on our way to a school outing. We took a group photograph, and Meera later copied the shop name from the photo to make her own text, saying 'That's my shop.' At school, she enjoyed participating in bank, shop and office games. I heard her pointing out confidently in the home corner 'travel agency' that 'this is the counter, you have to be on this side,' and refusing a friend's attempt to put her in the role of client, by saying 'No, I work man, I work girl, I work in here.'

Meera's mother described how her older daughter Pinal would play at filling in delivery and order forms in the shop, and was learning to take orders over the phone. Meera would copy her sister in role play at home, and often brought leaflets, coupons and stickers from the shop into the nursery, incorporating these into home corner play. Her games involved prices such as '1p' and '£4.50'. She also referred to other literacy practices associated with the shop, saying, for example, 'I'm going to Cash and Carry,' with a 'ticket' in her hand (she had been to the wholesaler's with her father). The National Lottery began during that school year; tickets were sold at small shops like Meera's, and this immediately figured in Meera's nursery roleplays. She designated her own texts, and shop leaflets, as lottery tickets, with remarks like 'You win £40.'

On one occasion Meera brought me a large envelope from home, inside which was a lottery ticket and a prize (a pen wrapped in silver paper), along with some leaflets from the shop. This was one of a number of envelopes containing messages and gifts which Meera arrived with at school in the morning, waiting excitedly to show the teacher and myself. Through this transfer of texts, Meera created a constant connection between uses of writing at home and at school. She felt confident about doing so because we were encouraging her to use collaborative play within the nursery to build on the knowledge of literacy and numeracy which she was gaining from her home world.

Relating to school literacy at home

Meanwhile, Meera engaged in writing activities at home which showed how she had identified key elements of school literacy practices, and was extending her participation in these through imaginative play. Her older sister was an important reference point for Meera in exploring the world of school. Their mother described to me how Meera, having seen her sister working on a school project, stated 'I want to do project.' Picking up a set of papers and putting them in a file, she then said 'I've done my project.' One day Meera brought into the nursery a sheaf of texts which she had written at home, referring to these as her project. Included in the bundle of papers was a printed title page for 'The Tudors', one of her sister's National Curriculum topics, on which Meera had written her own name. On another occasion, when Meera mentioned homework in the nursery, I asked, 'Who does homework?', to which she replied 'My sister and me'.

Her mother also commented that Meera and Pinal played 'school' together, with Meera liking to assign roles by saying 'You are Sharon (the nursery nurse), I am Helen (the teacher).' Meera would give verbal instructions that she had heard at nursery, and the games would involve writing. Meera came into school one morning flourishing a large brown envelope with a 'register' of the nursery children's names on, apparently written by her sister. Children were marked present or absent, and the envelope was completely covered with additional writing, including a noughts and crosses game.

Thus school roleplays were an integral part of a wide range of literacy activities in which Meera developed her knowledge of writing, aided by her sister.

Relating to Gujarati texts in school

At home, Meera saw her mother reading newspapers in Gujarati, and she recognised a copy of one of these in the nursery, carrying it round with her and saying 'mummy, mummy, mummy!' She also sat alongside her mother at home when letters were being written in Gujarati to the family in India, saying 'I'm writing a letter,' and doing her own wavy-line writing. She would write in a similar way when looking at a Gujarati magazine, saying 'I'm writing it,' and her mother would respond 'You can try.'

Both Meera's parents encouraged her writing at home, and she was being taught the English alphabet; Meera's mother explained to me that they thought it was too early to teach her to write in Gujarati as well, since this might be too hard for her. However, on the first occasion when her mother did some Gujarati writing in the nursery, Meera's reaction surprised us all. She climbed up on a chair to reach her mother's text, which was part of a display on the wall, and began to add her own wavy-line writing, saying 'I'm writing in Gujarati.'

At least ten times during that school term, Meera wrote a similar kind of emergent 'Gujarati', filling up the display text and producing separate sheets of her own (*see* Figure 6.1), while making statements such as 'I write like my mum.' The event of her mother being invited to sit down and write in the nursery seemed to enable Meera to connect with her home language at school, and to give extra impetus to her interest in Gujarati script.

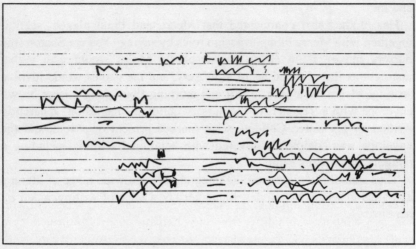

Figure 6.1   Meera's early 'Gujarati'. At this point she could write several letters of her name in English.

As she made her own marks next to her mother's, Meera mentioned 'fillums' and 'TV' several times. I wondered if she associated these with the Gujarati language, and her mother confirmed that the family often watched Indian film videos together at home. Although these were actually in Hindi, the talk around the television was in Gujarati, and when Meera brought her favourite video to school, the title was written in Gujarati on the spine.

The nursery children watched extracts from this video, involving singing, dancing and slapstick comedy, with great enthusiasm. Meera wanted to repeat the event of seeing her film with her peers at school, and, as I shall later describe, it was to become the basis for a considerable amount of literacy work on her part.

Meanwhile, towards the end of that first term, a Christmas postbox was set up in the nursery, and Meera's mother, amongst other bilingual parents, worked with Meera in the classroom to write cards to be 'posted'. Seeing her own name written in both English and Gujarati, and helped by

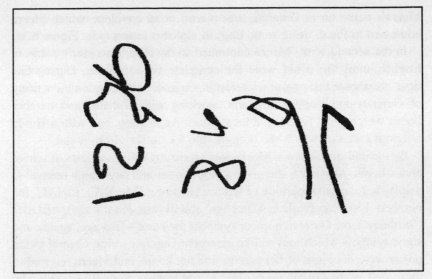

Figure 6.2   Card written by Meera: 'It's Gujarati – Pinu, my sister'.

her mother to copy the latter, Meera responded by making two texts for her sister. Significantly, she wrote in both English and Gujarati, just as she interacted with Pinal in both languages at home. One card was filled with separate symbols which differ from the English alphabet: of these, Meera said 'It's Gujarati – Pinu, my sister' (*see* Figure 6.2). Another card, with

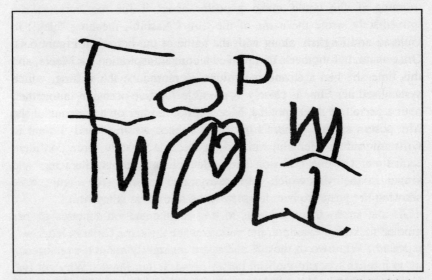

Figure 6.3   Envelope addressed to Pinal, including some English alphabet letters.

Meera's name on in Gujarati, was placed in an envelope which Meera addressed to Pinal, using some English alphabet letters (see Figure 6.3).

In the second term, Meera continued to develop her sister's name in English, until she could write the complete version alone. During this time, she showed an ongoing interest in Gujarati letters, and in the writing of Gujarati and English numbers, working with alphabet and number books which I had found in a local South Asian shop, and with a Hindu religious calendar which she brought into the nursery from home.

By the end of this term, Meera was producing bilingual texts at school and at home. At school, she made a large poster one day which seemed to display her current repertoire of written language: 'MeeRA', 'PINAL', the numbers 1 to 12 in English, 4 (her age) and 01 (ten, Pinal's age), ABDDD ('birthday'), the Gujarati number symbols for 1 and 4 (her age, again), and some symbols which looked like emergent Gujarati script. Central to the poster were drawings of her parents and her home, and Meera referred to these first when explaining her text to her teacher. Soon afterwards, she brought a collection of writing from home, including strings of English alphabet letters and several Gujarati symbols for 4. Thus Meera was choosing to represent concepts of key significance to her family and her home life, in both English and Gujarati.

It was at this point that Meera had the chance to bring her video to school again for a second showing. Sensing that this favourite film could provide further literacy opportunities, I asked Meera's mother one morning if she could make a poster about it for the nursery; she immediately wrote the name of the film ('Nashib', meaning 'luck') in Gujarati and English, along with the name of the hero (see Figure 6.4). Once again, her mother's text proved a crucial inspiration for Meera, and this time she had a strong motivation to reproduce the writing, which symbolised her film, as closely as possible. On five occasions altogether, over a period of three months, Meera produced her own versions of the film poster, saying 'Where's my mum's video writing?' and 'I want to write my video.' Her Gujarati writing became steadily more confident each time. On one occasion she added pictures about characters and scenes in the film which were memorable for her (see Figure 6.5); showing her poster to her classmates, she said 'This is my film.'

As she made these posters, Meera commented on features of her mother's text. For example, she noticed when the same Gujarati letter was repeated: 'Why two of those?' She asked insistently about the recurrence of an English letter in the film hero's name, Johan Janne: 'Why got two J's?' Although she did not yet refer to 'words', she wanted to know why some symbols were grouped together with a space between them: 'Why

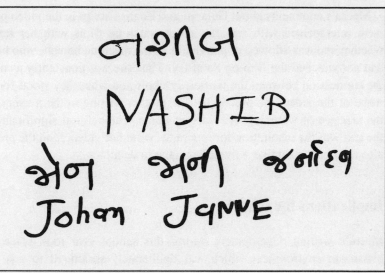

Figure 6.4   Poster by Meera's mother for the film 'Nashib'.

mummy done a gap?' She also asked 'Why three?', noticing that three groups of Gujarati letters (for the name of the film hero) seemed to correspond to only two groups of English letters. When I checked this with Meera's mother, she explained that she had not been sure how to write the third part of the name in English script.

Figure 6.5   One of Meera's film posters, with drawings of characters and events from the video.

Meera's comments about Gujarati and English script in the video poster were interspersed with remarks about watching films with her family: whether she was allowed to put videos in the machine herself, who had or had not watched the film on Saturday. Thus she was constantly aware of the connection between the written symbols and what they stood for: the name of the video, the practice of her mother writing in the nursery, and the practice of watching the video at home. The cultural significance of the text was the inspiration for Meera to 'write her video', and the process also led her to examine written language in detail.

Implications for schools

Meera's writing development during this school year took place in a classroom environment which was deliberately structured to link with children's knowledge of home literacy practices. This structuring was necessary for two reasons.

Firstly, school literacy work has tended to focus on certain genres of writing, with particular emphasis on narrative (Martin, Christie and Rothery, 1987). Whilst narrative is a significant genre in education and in society, children also need to develop texts for a wide range of social purposes, and work such as that of the National Writing Project (1990a, 1990b) has shown the success of using genres in school which relate to other aspects of everyday life (Czerniewska, 1992). In particular, the contribution of sociodramatic play to literacy development in the classroom has been emphasised by Neuman and Roskos (1993) and Hall and Robinson (1996).

The setting up of a home corner which facilitated children's interaction with print, and the teacher's recognition of the importance of texts which were used and produced there, was a key factor in helping Meera to draw on her experiences of reading and writing in the family shop and at home. She already had definite and highly motivating purposes for literacy in mind, which she was able to explore further with her classmates at school.

Secondly, school literacy work in the United Kingdom has tended to take place entirely in English. Under these conditions, bilingual children are unable to derive maximum benefit from the knowledge of literacy which they possess in their home languages. This knowledge is now thought to transfer between home languages and English (Edwards, 1995), and it has been acknowledged that multilingual work in the classroom can help children to understand more about how language works (DES, 1989).

For Meera, the possibility of working continuously in Gujarati alongside English was opened up by the integration of familiar home texts, and parents as writers, into the classroom. Integration meant that each home language text had a purpose which was part of the nursery curriculum. There could be a direct link with the current topic of study as when Meera's mother, along with other parents, translated part of a display on the nursery wall. When the topic was 'travel', several bilingual parents, again including Meera's mother, worked with their children to make pages about their countries for a travel brochure, in their home languages. Parents also wrote airletters to relatives in other countries, to ask for information and pictures for the travel topic. As well as writing a real letter to send from home, parents wrote shorter versions in the nursery, and children reacted by sitting next to their parents and writing their own airletters. This connected with the practice of family letter-writing at home, which several bilingual parents had described to me. In Meera's case, an interplay developed between the topic and symbols used in her mother's airletter and in her own.

Meanwhile, texts such as alphabet-teaching materials and calendars became part of ongoing classroom work on letters and numbers. Home language videos, of which Meera's was one, were watched in the weekly nursery 'video time', posters made by parents about the videos were displayed in the nursery, and in some cases invitations were issued to another class to come to a viewing.

Conclusion

While Meera was a particularly prolific writer, she was not unique in her positive response to the environment just described. Her classmates, including other bilingual children, also took up the opportunity to create their own texts based on literacy practices which they had participated in at home. Within the classroom, children could return to these texts and reflect on their content, and experiment further with written language, a process which was undertaken in considerable detail by Meera in her video writing.

Although school and home contexts inevitably differ, it is important for teachers to construct a 'home–school discourse', open to children's everyday literacy experiences, and to provide opportunities for multilingual writing, which can help children from different social and cultural backgrounds develop their literacy knowledge to its fullest potential.

References

Bissex, G. (1980) *GNYS AT WRK: A Child learns to write and read*. Cambridge, Mass: Harvard University Press.

Bhatt, A. and Martin-Jones, M. (1997) 'Literacies in the lives of young Gujarati speakers in Leicester', in Durgunoglu, A. and Verhoeven, L. (Eds) *The Acquisition of Literacy in Multilingual Settings*. Hillsdale, NJ: Lawrence Erlbaum Associates.

Czerniewska, P. (1992) *Learning about Writing*. Oxford: Blackwell.

Department of Education and Science (1989) *English for Ages 5-16*. London: HMSO.

Edwards, V. (1995) *Writing in Multilingual Classrooms*. Reading: Reading and Language Information Centre, University of Reading.

Hall, N. and Robinson, A. (1996) *Exploring Writing and Play in the Early Years*. London: Fulton.

Harste, J.C., Woodward, V.A. and Burke, C.L. (1984) *Language Stories and Literacy Lessons*. Portsmouth, NH: Heinemann Educational Books.

Heath, S.B. (1983) *Ways with Words*. Cambridge: Cambridge University Press.

Martin, J., Christie, F. and Rothery, J. (1987) 'Social Processes in Education', in Reid, I. (Ed.) *The Place of Genre in Learning: Current debates*. Victoria, Australia: Centre for Studies in Literacy Education, Deakin University.

National Writing Project (1990a) *Becoming a Writer*. Walton-on-Thames: Nelson.

National Writing Project (1990b) *A Rich Resource: writing and language diversity*. Walton-on-Thames: Nelson.

Neuman, S. and Roskos, K. (1993) 'Access to Print for Children of Poverty: Differential effects of adult mediation and literacy enriched play settings on environmental and functional print tasks', *American Journal of Educational Research*, **30** (1), 95–122.

Saxena, M. (1994) 'Literacies among Panjabis in Southall', in Hamilton, M., Barton, D. and Ivanic, R. (Eds) *Worlds of Literacy*. Clevedon: Multilingual Matters.

Taylor, D. (1983) *Family Literacy*. London: Heinemann.

Taylor, D. and Dorsey-Gaines, C. (1988) *Growing Up Literate*. London: Heinemann Educational Books.

Part III

From Five to Seven: Languages and Literacies in Homes, Schools and Communities

In Part Three, we move from pre-school to school, and literacy gains a new significance. Chapter 7 reminds us of the danger of literature suggesting a successful paradigm for the acquisition of literacy: a paradigm based often on the importance of story-reading by parents. Nadia, Imrul and Maruf do not participate in this practice at home, yet are reading well at school. How do the authors account for their success? One reason is surely their impressive array of home and community literacy activities. As in Part Two, we learn about the vital role played by mediators who initiate children into a sense of belonging to a particular practice. Nadia tells of reading nature books with her grandfather and science workbooks with her mother; Imrul attends Qur'anic classes and is just beginning to read Urdu; and Maruf studies English reading-scheme books with his sister in addition to his Qur'anic and Bengali classes. But just as important is the skilled teaching they receive at school. Close analyses of individual and group reading lessons reveal complex, yet similar, patterns of interaction based on the teacher's understanding of home practices together with a clear explanation of the school reading task.

Other studies in Part Three document the role played by friends, video stories and a support teacher in mediating new worlds. We see how the children all share in common three crucial tasks: getting a sympathetic listener or mediator; ensuring the possibility of experimenting and taking on new roles through play; and finding the opportunity to communicate and become a significant meaning maker in the new language. Such tasks are not easy and we feel for both authors and children as they struggle to learn from each other.

From Live to Screen: Languages and Literacies in Homes, Schools, and Communities

Chapter 7

Investigating literacy in London: three generations of readers in an East End family

Ann Williams

Introduction

Over the arched doorways two plaster figures, a boy and girl in 18th-century dress, look down over the children as they thread their way to school between the sober-suited ranks of city workers. A hundred yards to the right of the school, the gleaming glass and metal structure of the Lloyds Building and the soaring skyscrapers of the City; to the left, the Victorian tenements, built to house the poor at the end of the 19th century when the horrors of the Jack the Ripper murders had drawn the attention of the public to the appalling conditions of those who lived in 'the Great Wen'. The mothers gather around the gate, unaware that on this very spot in 1888 the Ripper's fifth victim was found, and shepherd their children into class where they settle on the rug: John whose parents are from Nigeria, Azad whose family is from Bangladesh; Wesley whose grandparents are in Jamaica; Sally whose parents have come down from Lancashire. Mrs Kelly, born in London of Irish parents, welcomes her class.

The school, founded by a philanthropic alderman of the City of London, has been educating children for almost three centuries and has seen whole populations come and go. In the 18th century, French Huguenots brought great prosperity to the area with their rich brocades and jacquard cloths until the invention of the power loom threw thousands of weavers into poverty and destitution. In the 19th century, the devastating potato famine drove the Irish to seek work here, constructing London's new railway system. Next came the Jews fleeing pogroms and persecution in Russia and Eastern Europe. As they established themselves and became prosperous they moved out to the suburbs, leaving the houses for families from Bangladesh. Now they, in turn, are beginning to move to the suburbs, making way for Somalis, Ethiopians and others escaping conflict.

Since the Middle Ages, this area bordering the City of London has housed the newcomers, the migrants in medieval times, those who were not allowed to take up residence within the city walls. For centuries the inhabitants have clothed, shod and fed the prosperous burghers of the capital. Today, living conditions are still cramped, residents suffer from ill-health caused by pollution and in the schools teachers have to cope with the effects of inner city deprivation and large classes in which most children speak a language other than English as their mother tongue.

This is an area which has recently been the focus of considerable attention. In 1996 an OfSTED report on reading standards on three inner London boroughs indicated that children in these inner city areas do not achieve as well as their counterparts elsewhere. Politicians and edu-cationists alike have been quick to lay much of the blame for poor literacy standards at the feet of the parents.

The importance of the pre-school home environment on children's subsequent literacy development has been recognised for some time (Wells, 1985). Literacy practices in the home, ranging from the bed-time story to parents' own reading habits, have been seen as crucial factors in predicting a child's later success in reading and writing. Parental responsibilities are wide-ranging. Parents' level of education has been seen as having a contributory effect and some bodies (Adult Literacy and Basic Skills Unit (ALBSU): 1993) have been uncompromising in attri-buting children's difficulties in school to parents' own poor literacy and numeracy skills. Cultural practices within the home are considered to have far-reaching effects. Story reading at the pre-school stage, for example, has been judged to be essential for equipping children with the skills 'which children have to learn if they are to participate successfully in such book-reading interactions' (Snow and Ninio, 1986:136). It has been suggested that some children have heard up to 6,000 story readings before starting school (Barton, 1994). Even the quality of the social-emotional bond between parent and child during the story reading has been considered to exert a considerable influence on a child's development with the result that 'insecurely attached dyads will have less rewarding and satisfying interactions in general and literacy interactions in particular' (Lesemann, 1996).

Research on early literacy, then, seems to point to a number of neces-sary conditions if a child is to achieve success in school. Much of the literature seems to suggest that there is a successful paradigm for the acquisition of literacy and that literacy will only emerge if 'conditions are right, ie contexts which support, facilitate enquiry, respect performance and provide opportunities for engagement in real literary acts' (Hall, 1987:10). Yet we all know exceptions to the rule: children from low income families, the sons and daughters of migrant workers, children in developing countries who, in spite of adverse conditions, achieve spectacular results. Large-scale quantitative studies (Wells, 1985 and Lesemann, 1996) provide broad overviews based on socio-economic and ethnic groupings, but do not furnish the details that enable us to explain the exceptions; those children who, in spite of what might be seen as a lack of propitious circumstances, appear to succeed as well as their more privileged counterparts. Studies of individual families permit the researcher to tease out the more subtle or hidden factors that contribute to successful early literacy, as the following case study aims to demonstrate.

The case study

Nadia was one of a group of children who took part in a study designed to investigate family literacy histories and children's learning strategies in the East End of London (Gregory, Mace, Rashid and Williams, 1996). Researchers worked with six families for whom English was a first language and seven families of Bangladeshi origin whose home language was Sylheti. The children attended two adjacent primary schools. The data collected for each child consisted of recorded interviews with family members, with the child's teacher, and with the child him/herself. In addition, classroom observations were carried out weekly throughout the school year, and each child was audio-taped reading with a teacher and at home with a member of his/her family. Nadia was one of two good readers who were also recorded reading with a younger, less fluent reader. The research combined ethnographic and ethnomethodological approaches, the focus of the study moving from the wide social context to detailed analysis of individual reading interactions.

It has been suggested that a child's progress in acquiring literacy is dependent on three principal factors (Teale, 1986:174):

1. Adult/child (or sibling/child) interactions which involve literacy.
2. The child's independent explorations of written language.
3. The child's observation of others using written language.

Teale's model provides a useful framework for considering the literacy practices of seven-year-old Nadia and the adults who shared her life.

Nadia's family background

Nadia lives with her mother and brother in a fifth-floor council flat in the East End of London. Her great-grandparents came to London from Poland in the late 19th century and settled less than half a mile from the flat where she now lives. Her mother, Mrs Turner, is unemployed and the family has little money to spend on toys, books or outings. An initial visit to the home reveals little in the way of literacy practices. The house is very tidy. In the sitting room there are no books visible, nor are there the 'artefacts relevant to literacy: newspapers, magazines, cookery books, notice boards, maps, encyclopaedias and dictionaries' (Leichter, 1984:41). There is little evidence of the vernacular literacy Barton (1994) suggests is present in most homes. Unlike other mothers involved in the project, Nadia's mother does not read for pleasure (Gregory *et al,* 1996) and, since she is currently unemployed, the children do not have the opportunity to observe work-related literacy activities (Taylor, 1983 and Teale, 1986).

Mrs Turner's own education was complete by 16 when she left the local secondary school. Although she remembers enjoying *Janet and John* books at home, she has no recollection of learning to read in school. Her happiest memories of her schooldays include playing on the school field (green fields and parks were also salient in the memories of other East End mothers involved in the project) and helping in the school shop. She feels that teachers' expectations for girls in the East End of London were low and they did not seem to care very much about the progress of their pupils. Mrs Turner played truant: 'I used to go home a lot of the time. My mum wasn't in and I just used to walk home.'

Although her parents were loving and kind, they seemed to have little ambition for their daughter and she feels they did not put enough pressure on her to succeed. Indeed, her mother objected to her applying for a place at a prestigious Jewish secondary school on the grounds that it was too far to travel. On leaving school Mrs Turner worked in shops and hotels in the West End of London until she married and had her first child.

Superficial observation of Nadia's family circumstances then show a very different picture from that of middle class homes such as those described by Schieffelin and Cochran-Smith (1984:6) in which 'the children were constantly surrounded by books and book-related items [where] children were provided with a wide variety of writing utensils, were encouraged to play with these materials and frequently saw adults using them.' Nadia, however, was just as keen and competent a reader as many children from more bookish homes. It was in the course of an interview that the role of other family members came to light:

A. Williams: Do you ever read any other books at home beside your PACT [Parents and Children Together] books?

Nadia: Sometimes I read these erm ...interesting books about birds and...

A. Williams: And where do you get them from?

Nadia: From my grandpa.

A. Williams: So there are books about birds...

Nadia: And books about plants and some about ants...

A. Williams: Are they interesting? Have they got pictures?

Nadia: Yes, but they aren't really like pictures like in a book what you read... like... just interesting.

A. Williams: Are they books for children do you think or are they books for adults?

Nadia: I think they're books for like seven to eleven year olds... But my grandpa's got lots of books... He's got all sorts of books about snakes, about birds, about insects...

A. Williams: Does he read them?

Nadia: Yes.

A. Williams: And where does he keep them?

Nadia: He keeps them in his wardrobe.

A. Williams: And what's your favourite one that he's got?

Nadia: I don't read that much but the one I read sometimes is this white book called *The Reindeer Book.*

A. Williams: Does he ever read to you?

Nadia: No.

Nadia's grandfather, like two of his brothers, had been a London taxi driver who, in order to qualify, had to pass the written examination based on what is often referred to as 'the knowledge'. His early interest in general knowledge has stayed with him all his life and even now, at the age of 80, he still reads widely and maintains his interest in subjects as diverse as stamps and medicine. As a father he had encouraged his own children, Nadia's mother and her sister, to read and to engage in literacy-related activities:

> He used to take me to WH Smiths in Elephant and Castle and buy me a load of books. I had some beautiful books.
> I used to love going to the library 'cos I used to go behind the counter and sort the tickets out. I used to love playing libraries.
> My dad bought me all those things.

His influence on Nadia is clear not only in her conversations about him but also in her choice of reading material. She spent one 30-minute silent reading session in school poring over *Flags of the World*, a reference book clearly written for adults, and one of her favourite home reading books was a children's encyclopedia.

Indeed, the crucial role played by family members other than the parents in supporting the child's reading was one of the unexpected findings of the research (*see* Rashid and Gregory, Chapter 8). One child had a new book every Thursday when she visited her grandma; another child had grandparents who bought atlases and other reference books she had encountered in school; and one grandfather taught his grandson to read using the sports pages of tabloid newspapers. It is clear that grandparents saw themselves as having an important role in the transmission of literacy practices and values. They clearly had the time and patience to sit with the children while mothers and fathers were occupied with other children or engaged in domestic duties.

Mrs Turner's own literacy history, however, has also shaped her attitudes towards her daughter's learning. While her own parents had encouraged her to enjoy reading at home, she feels that they did not put enough pressure on her to do well in school. She, like the parents in other studies (Taylor, 1983), now feels she must ensure that her children have the opportunities she herself missed.

> I put pressure on my kids. I want them to learn, even though they're young. I'll say to Peter 'What did you do in school today?' and he'll say, 'this and that', and I'll say, 'I want you to learn.' You know you want more for your children than you ever had.

As a result, Mrs Turner's attitude to literacy in the home is very different from the relaxed approach of middle class families described by Schieffelin and Cochran-Smith (1984:6) in which 'parents did not push their children to learn the alphabet or to practise printing techniques but simply assumed that their children would become literate and that their interests in literacy were part of normal child development'. Mrs Turner follows the pattern of many parents who see education as a way out of their present circumstances. Her approach to literacy tended to be instructive and formal, and was reminiscent of the Mexican-American parents in Reese and Gallimore's study (1996) in which 'reading with children centred almost exclusively around material sent from school.' She saw her role at home as complementing the work done in school by the teacher, Mrs Kelly who, she thought, was 'brilliant'. When asked about reading to Nadia she referred to reading the PACT books which the children brought home from school every night. She also showed me the *Language, Maths and Science Activities* book that she had recently bought at some considerable expense and which she and Nadia worked on at home. 'It's all reading you know. But besides reading it's got like questions... What has baby found? and so on... she's doing really well.' She also mentioned the *Collins Children's Dictionary* that Nadia was reading at home. 'It's got big letters... she really enjoys it... look, she's even got a bookmark where she's up to at the moment.' She has also bought a toy till and plastic money in order to help Nadia with her maths. 'It takes her a while to get into it but she does eventually. I think you've got to try and teach them yourself a bit.'

Mrs Turner's regret at not having attended a Jewish secondary school has also had repercussions on her children's lives, and she is hopeful now that both children will be able to attend Jewish schools. As a child she had attended Hebrew classes and visited Israel, but the declining Jewish population in the East End has led to the closure of synagogues and a lack of classes and community centres.

> I used to go in this.... near the library in J. Street. There used to be a small place and I used to go every Sunday to learn Hebrew. I was about 12 or 13 then. I used to really enjoy it because I could relate to people.

Thus Nadia's own literacy history is already being shaped by the histories of other family members. The influence of her self-educated and widely-read grandfather and the aspirations of her mother confirm that it is indeed 'the interplay of the individual biographies and educative styles of the parents' ... that become 'the dominant factor in shaping the literacy experiences of the children within the home' (Taylor, 1983:23).

Nadia's explorations of written language

It would be erroneous however, to ignore the role of the child herself and assume that Nadia was merely a passive recipient of others' attention. At seven Nadia is already an enthusiastic reader and writer both in and out of school. Moreover, she is confident in her abilities, a confidence boosted, no doubt, by her mother's faith in her.

> She was clever from a very young age. She could talk properly when she was two. She's always been very clever. She's fantastic at reading. She's brilliant. She read this book, *Angelina*, over the weekend.

Her teacher, Mrs Kelly, says of Nadia:

> Although she was initially insecure, she is now confident and in
> danger of becoming over-confident, and therefore needs monitoring
> lest she miss essential steps in her progress towards becoming a good
> reader.

Most of her out-of-school hours are spent indoors and with adults: her
mother, her mother's friends and her grandfather. She is at ease in adult
company and is a skilled communicator, responding appropriately to the
demands of the situation. She is her mother's companion and confidante.
Her view of literacy is based on her observations of adults and their
literacy practices. In her little room she keeps a writing set, envelopes and
paper.

> She'll sit in her room and she'll fold her legs and she'll write. She
> wrote my sister a birthday card. She wrote 'Dear Kathy, Happy
> Birthday, Best Wishes, love Nadia'... She asked me how to spell
> Kathy... but her writing...!

She also kept a diary and wrote stories:

> *Nadia:*   I write... sometimes I do stories. I've got a little diary
>   with Minnie Mouse on it and I write in there. Not every
>   day... sometimes.
> *A. Williams:* What sort of things do you write in it?
> *Nadia:*   What I do on Saturdays, what I do in school and what
>   we're watching.

Nadia's independence was clearly demonstrated in the taped home
reading session. Although it was requested that the parent and child
should read together, Mrs Turner gave me the tape saying that Nadia had
made the recording alone, reading the passage and operating the tape
recorder on her own. The following extracts suggest that she is used to
reading alone and attempting to make sense of texts independently. Her
teacher pointed out that she had maturity, good comprehension and word
attack skills, as the following examples taken from her home reading
passage demonstrate (the figures in parentheses indicate the length of the
pauses in seconds):

(a) After decoding and making sense of an unknown word (nighties), she subsequently remembers it correctly:

I hope you like the little dolls and their (2) *night (2) ies...,* love from Auntie J... (1) Joan. *Nighties* said Meg.

(b) She guesses from context:

She found an empty box with *a lie (3) lid.*

(c) She uses phonic strategies:

The next day mother cut some doors and windows with a (1) *rez...rez... raise... razor blade...* a cooking stove, two armchairs, some sssss (2) *stew... stools.*

(d) She corrects herself retrospectively in order to make sense of the text:

That afternoon, Mother and Meg went shopping, they found a pink bathroom set and when Mother saw a little set of *post and pans (3)... pots and pans* she gave them to Meg.

(e) She monitors her own comprehension:

Meg put a lot of things on the kitchen table: little boxes, paper ... *na paper nats...* I don't know that word [napkins].

(f) She appears to accept, however, that there are words that she can read but whose meaning she does not know. 'Larged' for 'laughed' occurred three times in her reading:

Mother larged [laughed]... (3) larged
Mother larged [laughed], I can see I am not going to get any work done.

(g) Her punctuation is still problematic:

'Oh', said Mother 'Who was in the kitchen putting away things?'
['Oh', said Mother, who was in the kitchen putting away things.]

Observation of Mrs Kelly's reading methods

It is evident that Nadia is an enthusiastic learner, observing adults around her and modelling her behaviour on their practices. Nowhere was this more evident than in the school context. Mrs Kelly, Nadia's teacher in year two was considered to be a 'brilliant teacher' by all the parents involved in the project. Mrs Kelly's methods were not based on any current orthodoxy, but rather on her 20 years' experience of observing children learning to read. Her stated aims in teaching reading were wide ranging: to instil a love of books in the child (she believed that children should see adults reading and enjoying books); to make the child feel happy and secure in the reading environment; to promote the idea that reading can be done in a variety of contexts, for different purposes and across the curriculum; to engender text-to-life experiences/life-to-text experiences and to provide a vehicle for children to talk about their own lives; to teach the child 'the language of books', that is, how books work; to persuade the children to become confident and discriminating readers by encouraging them to talk about the books they read. She felt strongly that the teacher should have a knowledge of the words each child knows at any one time so that she can say, 'look there's "and", the word we looked at yesterday', or point to the word when it occurs 'in other contexts such as on posters and wall charts'. The teacher, she maintains, should also know when to intervene in the child's reading and when to let the child try to work things out for herself

When we observed Mrs Kelly teaching and analysed the recordings of her teaching sessions, it was quite clear that she skilfully put her theories into practice. In the following extract she is reading with a small group of children. The school practice was for all children to read for 30 minutes every morning in graded reading groups. The class teacher, the Section 11 teacher, the headteacher and deputy headteacher each worked with a group of children in the class.

Mrs Kelly:	What made me think that I might like to choose this book?
Tope:	Maybe because Tony's in this school.
Mrs Kelly:	No, no... Why Tony Ross? Why did I think that this might be a good book? I'm not sure. But why did I think it might be?
Tope:	'Cos he's writ some nice stories.
Mrs Kelly:	I think he has. I've read some books by him before... some books that he has re-told and I've really enjoyed them.
Chris:	I think I've got a book at home by him.
Mrs Kelly:	Have a look at the title when you go home. See if you can notice it. Do you remember Mr... Oh I can't remember his name... he was working with the juniors. He used to love books by Tony Ross.

Nadia:	Oh I remember... I think his name was...
Mrs Kelly:	He went back to New Zealand... or Australia.
Tope:	Oh yes
Nadia:	I think his name was Ross.
Mrs Kelly:	Oh it was Ross! It was! It was! Well remembered! [laughter all round].
Mrs Kelly:	That was good... So before we read this story that he's re-telling who can remember the story of *Little Red Riding Hood*? Let's start with Susie.
Susie:	Well the mum made some cakes for her Nan...

In these opening moves we see Mrs Kelly mentioning her own and other teachers' enjoyment of books, using the 'language of books' by referring to the author and title of the book and the 're-telling' of the story, praising the child who remembered the name of the teacher and promoting a feeling of security in the little group by calling upon their collective memory of school life. She then gives the children an opportunity to express themselves in their own words before turning to the author's text.

The following three extracts show her guiding the group through the text. Her detailed knowledge of each child's repertoire and of each child's strengths and weaknesses enables her to prompt the children and consolidate what has already been taught. It is Susie's turn to read:

Extract 1

Susie:	[She] tickled the wolf on the nose. He opened one [beady eye]...'
Mrs Kelly:	[to the others] Now don't actually tell her this because I taught you. Do you remember? If you see the letter 'E' and the letter 'A' together... can you remember the sound?

Extract 2

Mrs Kelly:	This is quite a hard one actually and just to show you [pointing to picture] and it has to rhyme with 'peeling'.
Fatima:	Ceiling... ceiling.
Mrs Kelly:	I didn't know whether you knew that word or not. I'm sorry I gave you a clue now. And do you know what it begins with?
Fatima:	'C'.
Mrs Kelly:	Oh you *do* know. Well done. What did I think you were going to say?
Fatima:	'S'.

Although the children read in turn, the group reading sessions are a joint, rather than an individual, activity with a high number of turns per pupil. The children listen carefully to each other and are able to offer solutions to their friends' miscues within the safety of the group. It is the children then, rather than the teacher, who carefully scaffold each other's learning, while she guides the whole process and offers praise and encouragement, prompts where necessary and provides words when no one has a solution, making sure that each reader has time to work things out.

Susie is reading:

Extract 3

Susie:	Once upon a time, a little girl lived on the....
Chris and Nadia:	Edge! Edge
Susie:	of the forest. Her dad was a...
Tope:	woodcutter
Susie:	woodcutter...
Nadia:	whose
Susie:	whose...
Tope:	job
Susie:	job it was to...
Nadia:	hack
Susie:	hack down trees so that all sorts of things like houses... sorts...
Tope:	sometimes
Susie:	sometimes little...
Mrs Kelly:	Just a minute... sorry to interrupt you Susie [reading] like houses...?
Nadia and Mrs Kelly:	Go on two lines.
Nadia:	comics
Susie:	comics could be made from the wood
Mrs Kelly:	Good girl.

In this way each child has the opportunity not only to practise his/her own reading but also to listen to others and observe how Mrs Kelly tackled the teaching of reading.

In order to investigate the strategies the children might have acquired while working with Mrs Kelly, we asked Nadia to read with a younger, less proficient reader, Aisha. The following four excerpts are taken from the transcript of the 'lesson'.

Extract 1

Nadia:	Do you want this or this? [offering two books]
Aisha:	This [starting to read] Snow is falling...
Nadia:	Shall we read who it's by? [Expecting Aisha to join in] By Franklin M. Bradley. Illustrated by Holly Keller.
Aisha:	Snow is falling [Aisha hesitates, Nadia points to the pictures]
Nadia:	What is it there? [picture of night scene]
Nadia:	It's night isn't it. Night...
Aisha:	Night has come and ...
Nadia:	snow
Aisha:	snow it
Nadia:	is
Aisha:	is falling. It...
Nadia:	it
Aisha:	It
Nadia:	It falls

Extract 2

Nadia:	Try and do this one.
Aisha:	Er, er
Nadia:	This.... What's that say? You know snow don't you? So what does that say? Look at this [pointing to picture].
Aisha:	snow... snow... snowflake
Nadia:	Good!

The first two extracts suggest that Nadia knows about opening moves. She introduces Aisha to knowledge about books by insisting on reading the title and the name of the illustrator; she uses picture cues to help Aisha decipher the text and prompts and encourages the learner. At the same time she pays close attention to the text itself, providing words phrases when necessary, breaking down words, and reminding Aisha of words that have already occurred in the story:

Extract 3

Aisha:	and that's the...
Nadia:	wrong... wrong
Aisha:	wrong way to spread jam and the...
Nadia:	you just read it there
Aisha:	wrong way to ssss...
Nadia:	skip

Aisha:	skip, she said. It's the right way...
Nadia:	says
Aisha:	says George...
Nadia:	What did he say there? It's the same word as that – wrong.
Aisha:	wrong...
Nadia:	[yells]...

Extract 4

Aisha:	It's Monday again. You'd...
Nadia:	Look. See that says bet
Aisha:	bet...
Nadia:	and that says er. Put them together and they make...?
Aisha:	better play nicely (2) Jaws so...
Nadia:	says
Aisha:	says his mum.
Nadia:	Reme...mber – remember

Although only seven, it is clear that Nadia already has a good deal of knowledge, both about what it is to be a reader and about strategies one might use to decode the text. In order to quantify similarities and differences between Nadia's and Mrs Kelly's reading sessions the transcripts were analysed, and a list of the strategies used by the 'teachers' to respond to their 'pupils' miscues and guide them through the text was compiled. The categories were based originally on work by Hannon *et al* (1986) and later adapted to suit our data. Twelve strategies were identified which seemed to fall into two groups: 'modelling strategies', which aim to initiate the learner into being a good reader, and 'scaffolding strategies', which are used to support the reader in decoding the text itself. The former included imparting knowledge about books, relating the text to the reader's real life experiences, and using it to extend the learner's language development. The latter included using phonics, breaking down words and insisting on accuracy. The moves made by the 'teachers' in response to the learner's hesitations and miscues were allocated to one of the twelve categories of strategies and the number of moves in each category was expressed as a percentage of the total moves.

The results are shown in Figures 7.1 and 7.2 (see p.104). Mrs Kelly uses a balance of modelling and scaffolding strategies, with the seventh strategy, providing text, the most common (27 per cent of all moves). Nadia's graph shows similar results with providing text by far the most common. When Mrs Kelly's and Nadia's scaffolding strategies were broken down still further using Hannon et al's original categories (1986), the resulting graphs in Figures 7.3 and 7.4 (see p. 105) were strikingly similar. It would appear that Nadia has observed her teacher so accurately that not only is she now able to read well herself, but she can also reproduce Mrs Kelly's teaching skills in order to teach other children.

Conclusion

There are few professional families in the school sandwiched between the wealthy financial corporations and the council flats. Yet Nadia was not the only good reader in her class of 30 children. The group, reading so enthusiastically and fluently with Mrs Kelly, included a child whose parents had come to London from West Africa, children for whom English was a second language and, children from families receiving state benefits. In short, the class included children whose family circumstances might be seen to militate against their becoming good readers. Bedtime story reading and highly literate parents may be desirable ingredients in the recipe for successful early literacy, but they are not available to all children. A factor that has been largely overlooked in large-scale studies, but clearly described in smaller case studies, such as that of six year old Elsey, the Torres Strait Islander (Kale and Luke, 1991), Tajul, the four year old Bangladeshi origin boy (Gregory, 1996:50) and, very clearly in Nadia in this chapter, is the child as an independent learner, a seeker of information, actively basing learning on observation and determined to come to grips with literacy. This determination, combined with the skilled teaching of Mrs Kelly and support for the school's work in the home has meant that Nadia has embarked on a literacy history that will enable her to fulfil her mother's aspirations and, following the pattern set by previous generations of settlers in the East End, move on to a stimulating education and a successful career.

Acknowledgements

The research project *Family Literacy Histories and Children's Learning Strategies at Home and at School* (R000221186) was funded by the Economic and Social Research Council.

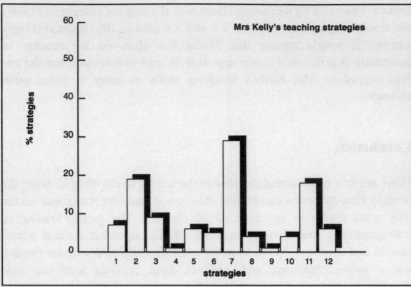

Figure 7.1   Mrs Kelly's reading with group: modelling and scaffolding
strategies

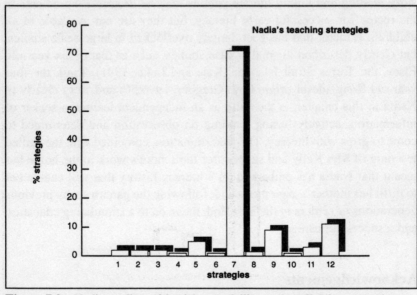

Figure 7.2   Nadia reading with Aisha: modelling and scaffolding strategies

KEY

Modelling Strategies: 1 Opening and closing moves; 2 Imparting knowledge about
books; 3 Positive feedback; 4 Negative feedback; 5 Text-to-life interactions;
6 Language development.

Scaffolding strategies: 7 Providing text; 8 Using phonic strategies; 9 Breaking down
words; 10 Establishing meaning; 11 Pausing and prompting; 12 Insisting on accuracy.

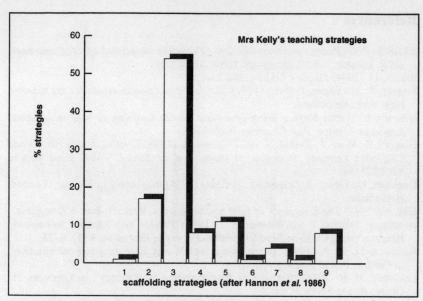

Figure 7.3   Mrs Kelly reading with group

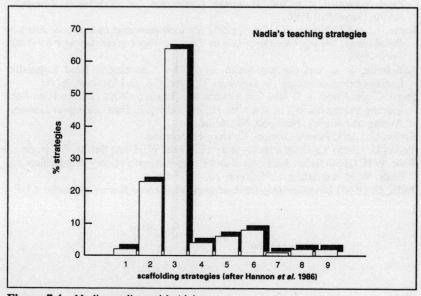

Figure 7.4   Nadia reading with Aisha

KEY
1 Negative comment; 2 Insisting on accuracy; 3 Providing whole words;
4 Pausing; 5 Prompting; 6 Splitting words; 7 Providing initial sounds;
8 Providing auditory clues; 9 Identifying phonic elements.

References

ALBSU (1993) *Parents and their Children: The intergenerational effect of poor basic skills.* London: Adult Literacy and Basic Skills Unit.

Barton, D. (1994) *Literacy.* Oxford: Blackwell.

Furniss, E. and Green, P. (Eds) (1991) *The Literacy Agenda: Issues for the nineties.* New York: Heinemann.

Gregory, E. (1996) *Making Sense of a New World: Learning to read in a second language.* London: Paul Chapman Publishing.

Gregory, E., Mace, J., Rashid, N. and Williams, A. (1996) *Family Literacy History and Children's Learning Strategies at Home and at School.* ESRC Final Report, R000221186.

Goelman, H., Oberg, A. and Smith, F. (Eds) (1984) *Awakening to Literacy.* London: Heinemann.

Hall, N. (1987) *The Emergence of Literacy.* Sevenoaks, Kent: Hodder & Stoughton.

Hannon, P., Jackson, P. and Weinberger, J. (1986) 'Parents' and Teachers' Strategies in Hearing Young Children Read', *Research Papers in Education,* 1 (1), 6–25.

Kale, J. and Luke, A. (1991) 'Doing Things with Words: Early language socialisation', in Furniss, E. and Green, P., *op. cit.*

Leichtner, H. P. (1984) 'Families as Environments for Literacy', in Goelman, H., Oberg, A. and Smith, F. *op cit.*

Lesemann, P. P. M. and de Jong, P. F. (1996) *Home Literacy: Opportunity, instruction, cooperation and social-emotional support predicting early reading achievement.* Paper presented at ECER (European Conference for Educational Research), Seville, September 1996.

Reese, L. and Gallimore, R. (Eds) (1996) *Ethnotheories and Practices of Literacy Development among Immigrant Latino Parents.* Paper presented in New York, April 1996.

Schieffelin, B. B. and Cochran-Smith, M. (1984) 'Learning to Read Culturally: Literacy before schooling', in Goelman, H., Oberg, A. and Smith, F. *op. cit.*

Snow, C. and Ninio, A. (1986) 'The Contracts of Literacy: What children learn from learning to read books', in Teale, W. H. and Sulzby, E. (Eds) *Emergent Literacy: Writing and reading.* Norwood, NL: Ablex.

Taylor, D. (1983) *Family Literacy.* London: Heinemann.

Taylor, D. (1986) 'Creating a family story', in Teale, W. H. and Sulzby, E., *op. cit.*

Teale, W.H. (1986) 'Home background and young children's literacy development', in Teale, W. H. and Sulzby, E. (Eds) *op. cit.*

Wells, G. (1985) *Language Development in the Pre-school Years.* Cambridge: CUP.

Chapter 8

Learning to read, reading to learn: the importance of siblings in the language development of young bilingual children

Nasima Rashid and Eve Gregory

Introduction

> 'He's a very sociable child, and he loves books
> he always brings them from school.'

Six-year-old Maruf is the youngest of five children and lives with his family in a council flat on one of the estates adjacent to the Petticoat Lane market in London's Spitalfields. Maruf and his siblings are second generation Bengalis, whose parents chose to come to Britain in the hope of a better quality life. Typically, his family comes from the lush green and picturesque region of Sylhet, a land-locked region in the north eastern corner of Bangladesh, an area which lies some 200 miles from the sea. Why then, should a significant number of Sylheti people arrive as sailors in London's East End, when they lived so far from the sea? In her book, *Across Seven Seas and Thirteen Rivers,* which depicts the lives of men who came from Bangladesh to settle in Britain, Caroline Adams (1987) suggests one explanation: a practice called the independent single tenure system whereby land was invested in those who worked it, which resulted in a class of relatively well-off small landowners. However, subdivision between brothers and sisters meant that plots became smaller until they provided insufficient sources of income. This left many families in a dilemma about alternative labour, since they claimed the status of Arab descent and would not lower themselves to engage in farm labouring in their own country. Furthermore, these men often were not educated enough to qualify for 'office jobs'. Gradually, the idea of working at sea became fashionable and increasingly difficult to resist because of the lure of money, adventure and admiration from local villagers.

Many believe that the relationship between Britain and Bangladesh is recent and although the first Sylheti men arrived only in the 1920s, the link between the seafaring Indian and London goes back to the times of Vasco De Gama in the 16th century. The few that settled in London at the beginning of the 20th century increased slowly until the 1950s, when there was a sudden influx of men demanded by the labour shortages brought on by World War II. By the 1970s the imposition of tighter immigration controls meant fewer new arrivals were entering. However, many were deciding to bring over their families, even though they had originally intended to be only sojourners who would stay a while before departing to their motherland. Sadly, the harsh reality revealed that many had not saved anything substantial to send back and, having been absent for so long, it would be difficult to set up again. More gravely, the onslaught of civil war swayed the majority into believing Britain would be a safer and more prosperous haven in which to bring up their young families.

The 1991 census shows that there are approximately 163,000 people of Bangladeshi origin in the United Kingdom. This accounts for just 0.3 per cent of the total British population of 55 million (Skellington, 1996). However, these figures tell us little about the area and school Maruf is attending. Maruf lives in the London borough of Tower Hamlets which has the largest population of Bangladeshi families in Britain (22.9 per cent of its overall population). Moreover, most families live in Spitalfields, an area of just one square mile adjacent to the City of London which means that, like some other schools in this area, all the pupils are Sylheti speakers.

Strong notions of patriotism and deeply-held religious views are entrenched in the minds of families in this community against the backdrop of what seems an alien host country. The community proudly upholds the traditions in which it believes. Simply taking a walk around the vicinity of Brick Lane will reveal many voluntary establishments set up for religious and cultural purposes where the reading and writing is in Arabic and Bengali. Maruf and his brother and sisters attend such classes for two hours daily after school and at weekends, a routine which is typical for Bangladeshi origin children in the area. But what is the purpose of such classes and how might Maruf experience them?

The Arabic class

It's a slightly blustery June evening when I walk towards the community building that houses the Arabic class of the once notorious Flower and Dean Estate. I am being escorted by one of the children's uncles who is the supervisor of this whole venture; a responsibility undertaken voluntarily as he works for the police force.

The surrounding area is quiet – deserted of all children, who, I presume, are inside the building. As I walk in I remember to cover my head. The walls do not reflect any of the work we from the western school would expect to see displayed. However this does not seem to hinder the children in their endeavours to reach the end of the assigned task.

In this particular class there are two male teachers, one of whom I discover is working with the more advanced children who are tackling the complicated word structures of the Qur'an. The other group consisting of younger children was in another part of the room with the other teacher, grappling with sounds and letters and oral verse. Everyone sits on mats swaying to the sound of his/her voice.

Although, on initial appraisal, the noise level may seem too high, relatively little of this is idle chatter. It is the expressed wish of the teachers that children read aloud, not only for them, but more importantly for Allah. Although English is very important for this life, Arabic is required for the life hereafter. Children are encouraged to develop an harmonious recitation in unison with the gentle rocking to and fro which accompanies the reading; they are told that Allah listens to His servants and is pleased if they take time to make it meaningful. I notice both teachers carry cane sticks which sway gently in the hand – a quiet but firm reminder that this is not a time to play...

Soon after the children gather closely together into their respective groups as it is time to recite prayers. I focus particularly on the younger members of the class, where the teacher in true pedagogic style paces before them waving his stick. He asks one child to recite the first 'kalimah', but is not satisfied with the response... he asks another, but still not good enough!

'Okay repeat after me!', he solemnly requests, 'Kalimah Tayyabh, la ilaha ilallaho, mohammadan rasolallahe'. He tells them to look at him as they repeat... I leave the room on the third recitation of the prayer and notice the children have not wavered at all; but remain seated on the floor as they have for the last hour and a half. (Rashid, 1996)

This pattern is reminiscent of children's Qur'anic classes in Morocco (Wagner, 1993) and may be common wherever reading of the Islamic Holy Book takes place. The purpose of learning to read the Qur'an is to please Allah as a follower of Islam. It is essential that one reads this in order to enter heaven. Although observance of the five pillars of Islam are necessary, the reading of the Qur'an forms the basic training on which to build further understanding.

The Bengali class

> Situated behind the Petticoat Lane market, this Bengali evening school is funded through the voluntary sector and comprises two mobile rooms. The room which I enter has several rows of desks at which children sit quietly – some writing copiously, while others practise words under their breath. The teacher sits at the front of the room. The walls are bare apart from a few information posters, some of which are made by the children and others not.
>
> It appears the mumbling from the children is practice of work from the previous lesson, because as the teacher passes around the room, the voice of the child on which he focuses his attention is momentarily amplified so he can correct if necessary, before moving on to the next.
>
> The children read one by one at different speeds; some at a great pace whilst others with careful deliberation. When he reaches the child I have come to observe, I see her read confidently and eloquently, although the few mistakes she makes are swiftly but firmly corrected. Parts that are not understood are explained thoroughly, but briefly, in Sylheti, thus the child's concentration needs to last for a considerable amount of time... and so the lesson continues in this way to the end. (Rashid, 1996)

The importance attached to learning to read and write in Bengali reflects the way members of this community value the written form of their language. Nineteen seventy-one heralded a new beginning for Bangladesh, as it elevated the language to national status, but through a bloody and treacherous war with West Pakistan (now known as Pakistan). On a more domestic level, literacy is the means of maintaining contact between children in Britain and relatives back home.

The picture of community learning given above begins to explain why children might transfer their experiences of reading from home to school. Both Bengali and Qur'anic classes share a clear and common pattern of interaction where the teacher demonstrates the task which the child practises through repetition before being tested. Furthermore, children focus on reading tasks for greater periods of time in contrast to time spent on work in the English school. Also, there are clear boundaries regarding the roles of both the teacher and the child. However, what seems to be of utmost importance is the high expectations teachers have of their pupils regardless of ability. Everyone is expected to finish the Qur'an and learn to read and write in Bengali, however long it takes.

Parents and children alike share the experience of these practices (Gregory, Mace, Rashid and Williams, 1996). Maruf's mother recalls how she enjoyed school although, like many, she completed only her primary education:

> I finished class 5... and then my mother died just after my engagement, leaving five brothers and two sisters, so I had responsibilities and from what I can remember everything was taught with a lot of rigorous testing and memorising.

As a result, parents like those of Maruf have transferred memories of their own experiences of learning to read to their expectations of the English classroom. However, the pattern of reading instruction in their children's school is very different from the one they remember, as we shall see later in this chapter.

The role of siblings

There is a plethora of literature that points to the significance of interaction which takes place between infants and caregivers. 'Knowledge itself originates within an interactional process. The child only achieves a fully articulated knowledge of his world in a cognitive sense as he becomes involved in social transactions with human beings (Newson and Newson, 1975:438)

Many researchers (Wells, 1987 and Rogoff, 1990) have recorded and analysed ways in which young children from all cultures and social backgrounds learn from their caregivers and, as a result, show teachers the value of what *every* child brings from home into school. However, although Maruf's mother talks fondly of schooldays and expresses great aspirations for her children, she also highlights the little time, skill and confidence she has in helping her children learn to read in a language which she herself is unable to speak.

What is different, but equally valuable, are the numerous literacy interactions that take place between siblings. Older siblings are mediators of the new culture for both their parents and their younger brothers and sisters. Jamilla is 15 years old and attends the local secondary school for girls where virtually all the pupils are of Bangladeshi origin. The school has built up a reputation for offering the solid education and support to see its pupils into higher education (several have qualified for Oxbridge). Jamilla would like to be a doctor and is very busy with her own school work at the moment. However, part of her responsibility is to sit with Maruf and read with him any books he brings from school.

They often read together before he goes off to his Arabic class, sitting informally in their small living room. Here they are reading *Don't Eat the Postman*.

Maruf:	Don't eat the postman. It was Tom...
Jamilla:	Tums –
Maruf:	Tum's birthday. Ram made him a birthday card. Don't eat the birthday card said Ram. But it is my birthday shouted Tum, I want some – I...
Jamilla:	Something –
Maruf:	Something to eat. Tum was...
Jamilla:	Saw –
Maruf:	Saw some beetles. Don't eat the beetles said Ram. um w-saw a [pause]...
Jamilla:	Rat –
Maruf:	Rat. Don't eat the rat said Ran.
Jamilla:	Ram –
Maruf:	Then Ram saw the postman. Tum ran to the door. Don't eat the police-postman shouted Ram. Don't eat...
Jamilla:	I –
Maruf:	I don't eat...
Jamilla:	Want –
Maruf:	I don't want to eat the postman shouted Tum. I want my box. Tum looked in the box. It's a birthday card...
Jamilla:	Cake –
Maruf:	Cake. Then There...
Jamilla:	They –
Maruf:	They have some cake and everybody was happy.

The tightly structured interaction between brother and sister reveals the complex nature of turn-taking in which they are engaged, and highlights the importance of strategies learned in both community class and school literacy lessons. Both participants begin in English as this is the language being learned. They focus entirely on the text (that is, there is no interruption with other book language or picture cues). Jamilla frequently corrects Maruf's mistakes as and when they arise, and has no fear of undermining his confidence. This example has a direct parallel with the explicit use of demonstration and repetition to which she has been accustomed in the Arabic school, where children are taught that the change of one sound can alter the meaning of the word.

Having finished the text in English, Jamilla begins to ask about the book in Sylheti:

Jamilla:	Bocho? [Understand?]
Maruf:	Kita? [what?]
Jamilla:	Story. [she turns to me – He's shy y'know]. Acha don't eat the postman manne kita? [Alright, what does *Don't Eat The Postman* mean?]
Maruf:	Ogo re? [this one?]
Jamilla:	Kita khore? [what does he do?]
Maruf:	Lettar post khore [posts letter].
Jamilla:	Postman manne kita? [What does 'postman' mean?]
Maruf:	Shobre sittee dhe [gives everyone letters].
Jamilla:	Tow ino kita oiyse? [so what's happened here?]
Maruf:	Thar baddey asel [it was his birthday]...

The excerpt from the Sylheti dialogue illustrates another pattern the children have experienced. As teacher, Jamilla needs to ascertain how much of the text Maruf has understood. This is a strategy she has borrowed from her Bengali class, where teachers always work through the written standard Bengali text using Sylheti. It is interesting to note how explicit her questions are. Rather than accept evasive answers, she will probe him on exactly what he means, and will further correct him if she is not satisfied. Only towards the end of the session does she use the picture to aid her questions, as she believes they do not always correspond with the text and 'might confuse the reader'.

To the outsider, her strategies may appear too probing for a young child, as she has not praised her brother at all for his endeavours, nor has she allowed him to 'enjoy' the book in the sense that many early years teachers in Britain understand the word. However, knowledge of the community classes allows us to understand that these children are very comfortable with such structures. Rather than feel under pressure from such explicit and specific demands, the children are challenged appropriately because they are aware of the high standards expected.

Going to school

It's a warm spring morning and the teacher has just finished calling the register, and is about to write the date.

Teacher:	Let's have someone do the date... [indistinct reply]... well done. Let's do it together – Uzma what was the date yesterday?
Uzma:	Tuesday, 27 February.
Teacher:	Good girl... and everybody... [children repeat]... lovely, and what will the date be tomorrow? Who can be clever...?

[A discussion follows about Eid, a letter and the new girl, Cynthia.]

Teacher:	Okay, let's find out what were doing today... [activities are sorted out]... okay, let's see who's sitting up nicely – everybody sitting beautifully...

[After some bustling around setting up places we find the teacher working with one particular group around shared reading.]

Teacher:	We're each going to read, so we'll start with Shanaz and you can read one page.

Uzma, who is a domineering child, not surprisingly intervenes, 'Point at the words'. Shanaz begins to read and gets stuck, there is a long pause and Happy is asked to help...the reading then continues, so that each child in the group has participated. This follows with a discussion about the pictures, at which point the teacher produces a worksheet around the text. The whole exercise has taken less than ten minutes, and the morning progresses in this slow, relaxed way. (Rashid, 1996)

   The teacher in the English school clearly believes that learning to read should be achieved through enjoyment, and children are often encouraged to choose books with this criterion in mind. Individual pleasure and self-expression are stressed and children are encouraged to voice opinions on texts from the very start of schooling. There is an immediate contrast between Maruf's community classes and home reading sessions, and his English school. Unlike Maruf's Qur'anic, Bengali and home reading sessions, there is no common pattern or ritual of repeating words correctly after the 'teacher'. From the excerpt above, then, we begin to see that Maruf will need to learn a whole variety of new strategies if he is to learn what counts as reading in his English class. More precisely, these new strategies are outlined below.

Independent reading rather than repeating after the 'expert'

Child:	[There] string.
Teacher:	String
Child:	String [pause] string on the upstairs
Teacher:	Upstairs

Similar examples show how the Bengali pattern whereby *the child repeats the correct answer after the expert* is actually reversed in school reading sessions. During school reading sessions, Maruf will need to learn that *teachers frequently repeat the child's response* and that this is a way of acknowledging its correctness rather than a correction; that it is a signal to continue rather than repeat the word again after the teacher.

Using pictures to interpret the text

Teacher:	Why did he put flour on the car?
Child:	[No response]
Teacher:	Why do you think he put flour on the car?
Child:	He was playing.
Teacher:	Playing? Why do you think he was playing?
Child:	[No response]
Teacher:	Pretending that the flour is...?
Child:	Snow!

Here Maruf must learn that the teacher is trying to encourage him *to interpret the text*, to question *why* someone might be doing something. Maruf is asked to identify with the character in the story and to try to predict what he might do – an approach very alien to his community classes and his home reading sessions.

Referring the text to real life events

Teacher:	Do you think it was a surprise – the jellybean tree?
Child:	Yeah.
Teacher:	Do you think he's happy?
Child:	Yeah he had a jellybean tree.
Teacher:	Do you like jellybeans?
Child:	[Shakes his head]
Teacher:	No? Have you had them before?

Child:	[Pause] nods her head.
Teacher:	You don't like them, well I do.

Again, Maruf must learn that 'reading' means discussion; in this case, relating the text to events in his own life.

Excerpts from the classroom show that the teacher frequently switches from text to talking around it, implicitly demanding a simultaneous reading of the text and personal opinions. These strategies do not come easily to Maruf. He does not elaborate on any of his answers and the teacher appears unsure of ways in which to support or extend his contributions. If we refer back to Maruf's reading with his sister, we notice that nowhere in the interaction was he expected to offer preferences or judgements; hence, perhaps, his lack of skill in using exploratory statements as he reads with his teacher. Rather than a lack of understanding as such, it seems most probable that the child is not used to this type of exchange which the teacher implicitly assumes he will share.

So how can teachers create a more effective learning environment which draws on practices that are known to the children, as well as introducing them to the new practices of school?

Bringing home and community to school

Work taking place in both adult literacy and school classrooms in the United States suggests benefits which accrue from drawing on 'funds of knowledge' available in the community (Auerbach, 1989 and Moll *et al,* 1992). A similar programme which aims to build upon existing knowledge and skills that children bring from home has been supported by the Paul Hamlyn Foundation in Maruf's school. Like many of the contributors to this volume, teachers in Maruf's school are questioning their own implicit assumptions about learning and devising ways to make their own understanding of tasks more explicit. Part of this process involves examining emergent bilingual children's strengths and strategies brought from home in order to build more systematically upon these in classroom lessons.

One practical approach has been to delineate more clearly the stages involved in learning to read and understand a text through 'structured story' (Gregory, 1996). Structured story simply divides story reading into stages which are easily recognisable by the child, and which are grounded on the advanced metalinguistic awareness shown by many young bilinguals (Ben-Zeev, 1977). Materials relating to each story (book, figurines for magnet-board, tapes, children's work cards, suggestions for teachers and, possibly, a video of children acting the story) are kept together in a story pack (usually a plastic folder).

The following stages show how the finely-tuned scaffolding of the older sibling can be taken into the classroom and used as a springboard for the type of discussion expected in school.

Stages in reading: *The Billy Goats Gruff* story

The Ladybird 'Read-it-yourself' version of this traditional European story was chosen because;
- The text was clear and straightforward and avoided the colloquialisms which exist in many modern reading schemes.
- The illustrations were brightly coloured and attractive.
- The text was one in a series of classic European tales which are cheap and easily available for parents.

The children worked through six stages in order to read the text with confidence.

1. Stage One: Telling the story

Initially the teacher told the story using magnet-board figurines based on illustrations from the book. Alternate telling in English and Sylheti enabled the children to make important parallels between both languages and gave them the opportunity to join in during refrains.

2. Stage Two: Acting the story

Research suggests that drama can play a vital role towards enabling children to understand the language of stories (Garvie, 1990) as it allows children to become totally immersed within the context. Children take on the characters of the story and also provide the dialogue. Acting the story provided opportunities to make costumes using the necessary language accompanying this.

3. Stage Three: Listen, discuss, do

To develop listening skills, children listened to short excerpts of the story on tape which instructed them to provide exact illustrations (for example, 'draw little Billy Goat Gruff standing on the bridge and the troll underneath it. Colour the goat brown and the troll yellow').

4. Stage Four: Across the curriculum

Work extended to other areas of the curriculum, for example, music, dance, art and craft.

5. Stage Five: Reading the story

Only at this point was the written text introduced, where the teacher read the story and highlighted individual words. Specific language games were incorporated at this level to build upon and strengthen the children's metalinguistic awareness. Key words from the story were written on to cards. Activities using the words included:

Word focus
The teacher removes a word card from view, and provides a description of word chosen, for example, 'what is under the bridge?' (for water).

Guess the word
This activity fixes the word in context in spoken language. A child secretly chooses a word and gives others clues to help them guess it, for example, 'goats like to eat this' (grass).

Opposites
This draws children's attention to important adjectives and prepositions in the story. A pack of 'opposites cards' are placed face down and one is chosen randomly by a child who must provide clues to the others, for example, 'it's the opposite of little'.

Emphasising intonation
Here the children read individual sentences chorally, individually or in groups after the teacher to gain correct pronunciation and intonation patterns.

Text-building
Children identify a single word in the text, and then read the whole sentence. This provides the opportunity to develop children's use of metalanguage, for example, 'word', 'sentence', 'full-stop'.

Picture description
Only at this late stage are children confidently able to describe pictures. The teacher begins by asking 'show me...' then 'tell me what is happening in this picture'.

Story-reading
The children are asked to read the whole story individually, in pairs or in groups.

Final story telling
The children now *tell* the story using only the figurines (in both languages, if possible) and the teacher tapes in order to analyse errors made.

6. Stage Six: Writing the story

Cloze Cards
Tasks asking children to complete appropriate words were set at various levels of difficulty enabling children to familiarise themselves with English syntax before they went on to write their own versions.

Story writing
This stage allowed the children to put to use the new vocabulary and grammar they had learned. The method of whole class shared writing (the teacher writes the children's suggested text and individuals gradually take over writing letters and words) as well as computer programmes such as *Talking Pendown* (Longman) were used.

Conclusion

In this chapter, we see how a detailed knowledge of children's home reading patterns can inform teaching strategies in school. We are gradually now accumulating evidence which suggests that Maruf's home and community class experiences may be typical for many linguistic minority children in Britain (Gregory, forthcoming). Maruf's family highlights the importance of older siblings rather than parents in his school literacy development. Siblings smoothly blend together strategies from community and school classes into a syncretic literacy (Duranti and Ochs, 1996) and, in so doing, act as mediators of the new host culture. They know from their own experiences that beginners to literacy in a new language cannot be expected to run before they can walk; school-like strategies are used only later when the child is confident enough to tackle them.

As teachers we have much to learn from a detailed examination of our own taped reading sessions. Do we recognise strategies used by different children and build upon them? How do we make our own interpretation of reading explicit to those who may not share it? Finally, if we recognise that children feel confident when they practice what they know (Cole, 1985) do we actually allow children time to practise in different contexts, and in the safety of the class or group, before we expect them to perform during individual reading sessions? Answers to questions such as these will say much in deciding the success of Maruf and his classmates in our classrooms.

Acknowledgements

This work was supported by the Paul Hamlyn Foundation (1993–4) and the Economic and Social Research Council (1994–5, R000221186). We should like to thank the families, schools and teachers in whose classrooms this work took place.

References

Adams, C. (1987) *Across Seven Seas and Thirteen Rivers.* London: THAP Books.
Auerbach, E.R. (1989) Toward a Social-Contextual Approach to Family Literacy. *Harvard Educational Review,* 59(2), 165–181.
Ben-Zeev, S. (1977) 'The influence of Bilingualism on Cognitive Strategy and Cognitive Development', *Child Development,* 48, 1009–18.
Cole, M. (1985) 'The Concept of Internalisation: Vygotsky's account of the genesis of higher mental functions', in Wertsch, J. (Ed.) *Culture, Communication and Cognition: Vygotskian perspectives.* Cambridge: Cambridge University Press.
Duranti, A. and Ochs, E. (1996) *Syncretic Literacy: Multiculturalism in Samoan American families.* National Center for Research on Cultural Diversity and Second Language Learning. University of California, Santa Cruz.
Garvie, E. (1990) *Story as Vehicle.* Clevedon: Multilingual Matters.
Gregory, E. forthcoming 'Siblings as Mediators of Literacy in Linguistic Minority Communities', *Language and Education: An International Journal.*
Gregory, E. (1996) *Making Sense of a New World: Learning to read in a second language.* London: Paul Chapman.
Gregory, E., Mace, J., Rashid, N. and Williams, A. (1996) *Family Literacy History and Children's Learning Strategies at Home and at School.* Final Report of ESRC Project R000221186.
Moll, L.C., Amanti, C., Neff, D. and Gonzalez, N. (1992) 'Funds of Knowledge for Teaching: Using a qualitative approach to connect homes and classrooms', *Theory*

into Practice, Vol. XXXI, (2), 133–41.

Newson, E. and Newson, J. (1975) Intersubjectivity and the transmission of culture: on the social origins of symbolic functioning. *Bulletin of the British Psychological Society,* **218**, 437–446.

Rashid, N. (1996) Field notes from ESRC Final Report, *op. cit.*

Rogoff, B. (1990) *Apprenticeship in Thinking: Cognitive development in social contexts.* Oxford: Oxford University Press.

Skellington, R. (1996) *'Race' in Britain Today.* London: Sage Publications.

Wagner, D.A. (1993) *Literacy, Culture and Development: Becoming literate in Morocco.* Cambridge: Cambridge University Press.

Wells, G. (1987) *The Meaning Makers.* London: Hodder & Stoughton.

Chapter 9

Friends as teachers: the impact of peer interaction on the acquisition of a new language

Susi Long

Kelli sat alone on the kerb in front of our house. One after the other, she picked up stones and threw them into the street. After a few minutes, she stood and walked up the hill to a deserted playground where she sat on a swing, climbed the rope ladder and played on the bars. Then she walked back to the kerb at the edge of our driveway and began throwing stones again.

Kelli was seven years old. She had just moved from the United States to Iceland and, more than anything else, she wanted a playmate. 'Where is everybody?' she asked when no other children came out to play, 'How come nobody's out?'

Eventually, neighbourhood children did come to play with Kelli and their interactions with her became the key to her adjustment in her new cultural setting. As the children interacted in the contexts of home, neighbourhood, school and extra-curricular activities, a supportive environment evolved which provided opportunities for Kelli to explore and develop an understanding of many aspects of her new world.

Kelli is my daughter. She is American by nationality but, at the time of our move to Iceland, she had lived overseas for all but two years of her life. Her father and I were teachers working for American schools, positions which led us first to northern Germany where Kelli was born, then to the Netherlands and, seven years later (after a two-year sabbatical in the United States), to Iceland. We arrived in Iceland on 21 August, 1991, one month before Kelli's eighth birthday. For the next nine months, I observed Kelli at the Icelandic school she attended, at home as she played with Icelandic friends, and as she participated in extra-curricular and community activities. I listened and questioned as she talked about the joys and struggles of her new life. Formally and informally I talked to Kelli's teachers, friends, and parents of friends about her experiences. Video tape, audio tape, hand-written field notes and a collection of school work, artifacts from informal play, letters and stories provided insights into Kelli's experience and allowed me to make important contrasts and connections concerning the process of her new cultural learning.

This chapter focuses on Kelli's interactions with three Icelandic girls and the impact of their interactions on the development of a system of communication and Kelli's acquisition of Icelandic. Accordingly, it asks what might be learned from Kelli's experiences in terms of the second-language students in our classrooms.

Kelli's Icelandic peers

Birna, Elva and Guðbjörg were Kelli's first and best friends in Iceland. They lived within walking distance of our house and were Kelli's classmates at the local school. The girls spoke Icelandic, a language that has changed little since it was brought to the island by Norse/Celtic adventurers in the 10th century. As is typical of many Icelandic seven and eight year olds, they recognised a few English words (picked up from watching subtitled American and British television programmes). Kelli met the girls when we visited their neighbourhood and school during previous visits to Iceland.[1] Two days after we moved there they initiated contact and, for the next nine months, Kelli played with one or more of them almost every day.

Kelli and her peers develop a system of communication

At about 8 o'clock on the evening of our second day in Iceland, the doorbell rang. Kelli and I opened it to find two girls – Elva and Birna – standing on the front porch. They were wearing roller skates. In a carefully-memorised English sentence (taught by her father for the occasion), Elva asked Kelli, 'do you want to play?' Kelli nodded, put on her skates and followed the girls outside. Rather than attempting speech or even gestures, the girls simply skated up the hill to the playground and Kelli followed them. Then they skated back to our driveway where they

---

1   Kelli's father moved to Iceland a year before Kelli and I joined him there. During that year, we travelled to Iceland twice for three-week visits.

stood looking at one another, smiling and giggling. Their smiles and giggles seemed to be nervous reactions to one another but, just as a mother responds to her baby's coos, the girls took turns in a sort of giggling proto-conversation and thus established potential for further communication.[2]

Several days after their first encounter, Kelli looked out of her bedroom window and saw the girls skating in front of our house. She hurried to join them and, as before, they smiled and giggled and skated up the hill. Later, Kelli led the girls into our kitchen and poured out glasses of juice for them. As she threw the empty juice carton into the bin, Kelli wrinkled her nose from the smell of the rubbish and giggled. The girls also wrinkled their noses and giggled. Then Kelli looked around the room and spotted the cooking timer. She turned the dial to make the timer ring and laughed a strangely artificial laugh. More forced than a natural giggle and more assertive than a reaction to something humourous, the exaggerated laugh seemed to be a way for Kelli to establish her place as a communicative member of the group. Elva and Birna laughed in response. By that point, the construction of a system of communication was well under way. With giggles and laughter as early strategies, and roller skates, the rubbish bin and a cooking timer as first resources, the children were making interaction possible. As described in the following paragraphs, their system quickly expanded to include intonated sound, facial expression, gesture, mime, invented words, 'foreignised' English, and abbreviated English.

After finishing their juice, Kelli led the girls upstairs to her bedroom where Elva and Birna walked from bookshelf to desk to bed examining the artifacts of Kelli's world: dolls, cuddly toys, photographs, and desk trinkets. They did not verbalise but continued to smile and giggle until Elva spotted a calendar hanging on Kelli's wall. She indicated her birth date and said, 'me Happy Birthday'. Then she noticed Kelli's globe and pointed to Iceland saying, 'Ísland' (Iceland). At the same time, Kelli looked for something that they could play together. Rummaging through her toy cupboard she considered and rejected several games and toys until she found a puzzle made of illustrated wooden cubes. Kelli put the puzzle on the floor and sat down beside it. Elva and Birna joined her and the girls began picking up puzzle pieces and trying to fit them together.

'Hmmm', said Birna as she examined a puzzle piece and shook her head. Then Kelli picked up a puzzle cube, tested possibilities for its

2 Jerome Bruner (1983) writes about proto-conversation as the type of communication that takes place between infant and mother (or primary caregiver) as they develop a 'predictable format of interaction that can serve as a microcosm for communicating'. (p.19).

placement and said, 'mmmm. mmm'? Raising her eyebrows as well as her tone of voice, Kelli gave meaning to the sounds and seemed to say, 'I wonder where this goes. Here maybe?' She tried to place the cube again, this time deepening her voice and furrowing her brow as she said, 'hmmmm'. The girls continued to work on the puzzle in this way, communicating by raising eyebrows, frowning, grinning and using 'mmms', 'hmms', and an occasional 'ah' as they added intonated sound and facial expression to their communicative repertoire.

Although Kelli and her Icelandic peers did not share fluency in either Icelandic or English, their first interactions were also typified by the use of words. The language they utilised ranged from Kelli's 'foreignised' English and invented words to the use of simplified English. When putting together the puzzle, for instance, Kelli leaned forward to place a puzzle cube and said, 'thay-errr' with an exaggerated 'ay' and a roll to the 'r'. It seemed to be a foreignisation of the English word 'there', Kelli's attempt to move away from her native language, or perhaps her perception of how the Icelandic girls might pronounce and, therefore better comprehend, the word. During the first days, Kelli foreignised many English words as she played with the girls. Among others she used 'mo-uh' for more, 'shih' for she, 'wahm' for warm, 'fust' for first, and 'den' for then. Within a few weeks, Kelli's differently-accented words moved further away from English and began to reflect her growing familiarity with the sounds of Icelandic. Instead of saying, 'better' and 'here' for instance, Kelli said, 'baytar' and 'hehtah' which were closer to the Icelandic 'betra' and 'hérna'[3] than to their English equivalents. She seemed to be striving not only to facilitate communication but also to sound as much like her peers as possible.

Kelli also invented words as she attempted to communicate. In the first play episode, for example, she placed a puzzle piece and said, 'Da' ('there'). Several days later, as Kelli and Birna arranged marbles into long rows, Kelli pointed to the marbles one at a time and said, 'da, da, da, da, da, da'. Later the same day, Kelli and Birna were playing with large cardboard blocks and, directing Birna, Kelli pointed to a block and then to a spot on the floor saying, 'dee dere' meaning, 'put that one over there'. Words like 'da', 'dee', and 'dere' did not approximate their English or Icelandic equivalents. They were Kelli's inventions that, again, seemed to be attempts to move away from her native language toward something that she perceived to be more comprehensible to her Icelandic peers. Immediately, Kelli's invented words were picked up by Birna, Elva, and

---

3   The Icelandic words, betra and hérna are pronounced, 'beh-trah' and 'hee-ert-nah.'

Guðbjörg and, as illustrated in the following excerpt from block-play, early interactions were often dominated by inventions:

Birna:	Okay. Dis, dis, dis. [Pointing to blocks.]
Kelli:	No. Dere. [Pointing to a space for a block.]
Birna:	Yes. [Nodding.]
Kelli:	No, no, no, no. Now dat. [Pointing to another block].
Birna:	Dis. Dat. Kelli, dis. [Pointing to a block and a space to place it.]

The use of invented words was effective but short-lived. 'Da', 'dis', 'dere' and so on were replaced by another strategy that also had its origins in their first evening of indoor play. Spotting her birthday on Kelli's calendar, Elva had said, 'me Happy Birthday'. A few minutes later, as they worked on the puzzle, Elva and Birna used more words from their limited English vocabulary ('yes', 'no', 'me', 'this'). They also used several Icelandic words, *'já'* (yes), *'hér'* (here), and *'svona'* (like this). At that point, rather than picking up the simple Icelandic, Kelli responded by using the same few words of English. Two days later Kelli tried more complex English sentences but, when the girls' responses indicated a lack of comprehension, she reduced the use of her native language to the five or ten words they had in common. Soon this abbreviated English became a standard method of verbal communication. Typical of their conversations at that time is the following exchange. It took place as the girls played 'mummies' and indicated their choice of dolls.

	Abbreviated English	Intended meaning
Kelli:	No me this.	I am not playing with this doll.
Birna:	No me this.	I am not playing with this doll.
Kelli:	Me this and me this.	I'll play with these two dolls.
Birna:	And me this.	And I'll play with this one.

At the same time Kelli and her playmates also discovered that, by using mime and gesture, they could support and extend the use of abbreviated English. This made it possible to express more complex ideas without the need for an extensive common vocabulary. Typical of their use of these conversational strategies is a discussion that took place in September, not long after we arrived in Iceland, in which the children 'talked' about musical instruments. Kelli initiated the discussion as she pointed to herself, pretended to play a piano and said, 'me la la la la la la'. Guðbjörg responded by pretending to play a recorder and saying, 'me doo doo doo doo'. Then she added, 'Elva doo doo doo doo'. Moving her fingers along an imaginary recorder, Kelli asked, 'Birna doo doo doo doo?' to which Guðbjörg replied, 'no. Me doo doo doo doo doo and Elva doo doo doo doo and Birna *var*[4] doo doo doo doo.' By supporting words and sounds with mime, the meaning of the conversation was clear:

Kelli:	I play the piano.
Guðbjörg:	I play the recorder and Elva plays the recorder.
Kelli:	Does Birna play the recorder?
Guðbjörg:	No. I play the recorder and Elva plays the recorder and Birna used to play the recorder.

Throughout Kelli's first four months in Iceland, the children almost always sought, and depended on, mutually familiar activities and objects (such as the roller skates, cooking timer and puzzles of their first evenings of play) to initiate and sustain interactions. For instance, during the second week, Kelli opened a photograph album and, showing it to Birna, pointed to photos saying, 'my father, my mother, my grandfather'. Birna extended the interaction by picking up an illustrated coaster from the coffee table, pointing to the illustrations of men and women and asking, 'is grandfather? is mommy'? In another instance, Kelli described the route we travelled from the United States to Iceland by using maps illustrated on place mats. Sitting with Birna at our lunch table, Kelli pointed to North America on her place mat map and said, 'Me here'. Then she moved her finger through the air saying, 'I go shooooo [flying sound] here,' landing her finger in Iceland. Birna asked for confirmation by retracing Kelli's route and saying, 'Kelli, you *kom* (come)?' Kelli nodded and 'flew' her hand across the map again saying, 'shoooooooo'. Similarly, long before they had a verbal language in common, Kelli and Guðbjörg sustained play for almost 20 minutes using a deck of cards. Unable to ask for cards by naming them (as in, 'do you have any threes?'), the girls revised the rules of the game to accommodate their communicative needs. They spread the cards face up on the table and pointed to them. Other resources that supported interaction included craft materials (paper, paint, coloured markers), board games, balls, dolls, cuddly toys, puppets, books, and musical instruments.

---

4   'Var' is the Icelandic word for 'was'. In this case, Guðbjörg used it to indicate that Birna 'used to' play the recorder.

The communicative strategies and resources described in the preceding paragraphs were utilised to facilitate interaction at a time when Kelli and her friends did not share a common language. Experts at their own system, the girls rarely hesitated between word, sound, and gesture. The use of one strategy flowed into another almost as smoothly as if they were speaking their native languages. At the same time, the construction of a communicative system laid the groundwork for Kelli's acquisition of Icelandic. As she used laughter, facial expression, gesture, mime, invented words and simple English to interact with Birna, Elva, and Guðbjörg, Kelli observed their use of Icelandic with one another. Thus, she heard the language used in the contexts of activities which she found purposeful and enjoyable and in which she was a motivated participant. Equally important was the fact that, as the girls constructed their communicative system, they created an environment which encouraged experimentation, a condition that would be essential to Kelli's eventual acquisition of the new language.

Kelli begins to use Icelandic

From studies of first language acquisition we understand the development of language to be an interactive phenomenon, a negotiation between two parties (Bruner, 1983 and Wells, 1986). Russian psychologist, Lev Vygotsky introduced the notion of the more knowledgeable partner as critical to the acquisition of language: the success of the partnership stemming from one participant's knowledge of the language and the other's desire to join a communicative world (Wertsch, 1985). Second-language researchers echo interaction-based theories by describing the role of the native speaker as critical to the acquisition of a new language (Ellis, 1985; Genishi, 1989; Hakuta, 1986; Long, 1987; Rigg and Allen, 1989; Wong-Fillmore, 1976, 1986). In second-language acquisition as well as first, the learner and the knowledgeable partner interact with one another in the negotiation of meaning (Ellis, 1985 and Wells, 1986).

Kelli certainly expected as much from her new cultural experiences. She wanted to become a part of a communicative world and she expected to reach that goal through interaction within that world. Kelli described this perspective saying that she would learn Icelandic 'by listening to other people'. She later added, 'You'd have to talked too. You can't just go, "mmmmm".'

Kelli's words accurately describe the impact that involvement with native-speaking peers had on her acquisition of Icelandic. Play-based activities with friends provided a comfortable setting as well as a motivation for experimentation and it was through comfortable, purposeful, supported experimentation that Kelli eventually acquired an understanding of grammatical structure, vocabulary, pronunciation, and appropriate usage.

I first observed Kelli using Icelandic during our fourth week in Iceland. She was directing Guðbjörg as they played *Mömmó* ('mummies') and she said, *'þú kom'* ('you come'). This first utterance was a literal translation of an abbreviated English phrase that had been in standard use. As Kelli continued to try the language, her utterances were often combination sentences: when she did not know the Icelandic equivalent, she used an English word. For example, 'Not this' became, *'ekki* this'. Through October, although Kelli was sometimes able to construct completely Icelandic phrases such as *'ekki núna'* ('not now'), simple English continued to be useful for clarifying and completing most messages such as, *Þú* help me *og Elva með þetta* (You help me and Elva with this). Also typical of Kelli's first Icelandic was the use of phrases frequently uttered by her playmates to one another. When I asked how she had learned *'sjáðu'* ('look'), for example, Kelli said, 'everybody says it . . . I just heard *sjáðu* something like that.' Similarly, she explained that she knew the exclamation, *'Hættu þessu!'* because, 'everybody says it when they don't want people to do things.'

From late September, Kelli rapidly incorporated Icelandic vocabulary into every interaction with peers as they played together. By mid-October, Icelandic dominated her play-based utterances and Kelli used the language with abandon, whether or not she was certain she was using it correctly. The following conversation between Kelli and Guðbjörg clearly demonstrates the opportunity for experimentation that informal interactions with peers provided. In the role of 'mother,' Kelli was trying to convince her baby (Guðbjörg) to sleep. Over and over, in an environment in which she felt at ease and had opportunity, time, motivation, and the resources to do so, Kelli reworked her construction of Icelandic in an attempt to say, 'If you don't sleep, you will not get any ice cream'.

	Icelandic	Translation
Kelli:	Sofa krakki.	Sleep child.
Guðbjörg:	Má ég fá ís?	May I have ice cream?
Kelli:	Kannski, á eftir þú sofa.	Maybe, after you sleep.
	Góða nótt.	Good night.
Guðbjörg:	Ég gét ekki sofa.	I can't sleep.

Kelli:	Sofa. Prófa. Prófa sofa.	Sleep. Try. Try sleep.
Guðbjörg:	Ég gét ekki sofa.	I can't sleep.
Kelli:	Prófa. Ekki ís	Try. No ice cream
	á eftir.	after.
	Þú ekki prófa, ekki	You not try, not
	ís.	ice cream.
	Þú ekki prófa, þú ekki	You not try, you not
	ís.	ice cream.
	Þú ekki sofa, þú ekki	You not sleep, you not
	ís.	ice cream.
	Þú má ekki ís	You may not ice cream
	á eftir þú ekki sofa.	after you not sleep.

Using Icelandic in play-based peer interactions not only provided opportunities for experimentation but, in that environment, peers provided specific forms of support that helped Kelli judge the success of her experiments and adjust accordingly. For example, friends often supplied words when a need was evident. Elva did this when she and Kelli baked a cake in late December. Kelli mimed the cutting of the cake and said, 'Við svona með hnifur' (We [cut] *like this* with knife). Supplying the missing word for 'cut', Elva simply said, '*skera*' and Kelli used the word in her next utterance: '*skera svona og svona*' (Cut like this and like this). Peers also rephrased their utterances when Kelli did not understand them, as when Kelli and Guðbjörg were making a picture out of plastic pegs and Guðbjörg clarified the word '*ramma*' (frame):

	Icelandic	Translation
Guðbjörg:	Eigum við ekki að hafa	Aren't we going to have
	ramma?	a frame?
Kelli:	Hah?	Huh?
Guðbjörg:	Svona rammi. Þetta	Like a frame. It is
	mynd þá	a picture then
	kemur svona	comes like this
	utanum.	around it.

Other peer support included simplifying and then extending the complexity of their Icelandic to accommodate Kelli's growing understanding of it; responding to Kelli's direct requests for help; direct teaching; allowing Kelli to reciprocate by teaching English words and phrases; and engaging in language play (using sing-song, rhyming, chanting, creating nonsense words), which allowed Kelli to rehearse pronunciation, vocabulary and usage.

The impact of peer interaction on Kelli's language development is probably best illustrated in a discussion of her acquisition of grammatical knowledge. At school, Kelli's language and literacy programme did not include lessons in feminine and masculine word forms, verb-noun complements, singular and plural, and possessives. At the end of her first school year in Iceland, however, Kelli had not only developed an awareness of the existence of those forms but was also consistently correct in her use of many gender-governed forms, prepositions, possessives, and plural and singular noun-verb complements. Clearly, the most significant arenas for learning the grammatical structure of the language were her play-based interactions with friends. At play with friends, Kelli enjoyed an environment in which was built an awareness of the existence of different word forms. In the same environment, she was comfortable enough to experiment with the use of those forms until, through feedback from peers and repeated exposure to correct usage – 'Elva said it one time and I heard Birna say it to Elva' – she began using correct forms consistently. From early November, I observed such experimentation as she alternated, seemingly indiscriminately, between correct and incorrect usage. Playing 'schools' for example, Kelli experimented with the use of gendered forms of words as she inconsistently matched feminine and masculine nouns and pronouns with complementary verbs. In the role of 'teacher', Kelli called the students' names:[5]

	Icelandic	Translation
Kelli:	Fridrick Þor (m).	Fridrick Þor.
	Er hann (m) veik (f)?	Is he sick? [incorrect]
Elva:	Já.	Yes.
Kelli:	Guðbjörg (f).	Guðbjörg.
	Hvar er hún (f)?	Where is she? [correct]
Elva:	Veik (f).	Sick.
Kelli:	Gisli (m).	Gisli.
Elva:	Veikur (m).	Sick.
Kelli:	Lilja (f).	Lilja.
	Er hún (f) veikur (m)?	Is she sick? [correct, incorrect]

5   In this excerpt, '(m)' indicates that Kelli has used the masculine form of a verb or noun and '(f)' indicates the use of a feminine noun or verb form.

As she played with friends, Kelli experimented with Icelandic in this way from her second month in Iceland. At school, where lessons were usually taught to the class as a whole and written work consisted predominantly of short-answer worksheets, Kelli did not experiment with the language. Except when interacting informally with friends (on the playground, whispering at their seats), she did not use Icelandic regularly in the classroom until the sixth month, waiting until she was certain she would be correct before attempting to speak.

By the end of May (the eighth month), Kelli was comfortable and proficient enough with Icelandic to use it to initiate, lead and organise play-oriented activities. Although her use of the language was not always correct, she had amassed a sizable vocabulary as well as an understanding of many grammatical forms and she used the language without hesitation. Clearly, the most supportive arenas for her construction of that knowledge were play-based interactions with peers. In that environment, Kelli learned vocabulary, sentence structure, grammatical form, pronunciation, and appropriate usage as she observed, listened, experimented, received feedback, assessed, adjusted, discarded, adopted, and extended her knowledge. By doing so, she continually evaluated language use in terms of its effectiveness in the native-speaking world in which she wanted to belong.

Conclusion

What do these experiences mean in terms of the second-language children in our classrooms? Certainly, we all recognise that no two cross-cultural experiences are the same. They differ in terms of family background, support systems, native language proficiency, personality, age, cultural traditions, school and community situations, and in countless other ways. Common, however, to many second-language experiences is the impact of meaningful interaction. Over and over we see children learning language as they interact with native-speaking peers: a five-year-old Chinese boy in America (Huang and Hatch, 1978), a class of 15 year olds in a British school (Burgess and Gore, 1990); Mexican children in an American setting (Wong-Fillmore, 1986), and five year olds on a London playground (Hester, 1984). At the very least, Kelli's story suggests the same: that peer interaction is supportive of language learning. At the same time, by focusing on the day-to-day experiences of one child, this study provides a close look at conditions that made peer interaction effective.

The first, and probably most significant condition supporting Kelli's language learning was the desire to interact. Kelli and her peers wanted to play. Second, they approached associations with one another assuming that interactive play was possible. Basic to that assumption was Kelli's expectation that she would eventually learn the language of her peers and would do so through interactions with them. Third, because she played with peers for several hours almost every day, Kelli had the opportunity and plenty of time to work through understandings about language. Fourth, the children's interactions were successful largely because they were supported by the children's interest in activities that were mutually comprehensible, purposeful and enjoyable. Fifth, resources (such as games, puzzles, bikes, balls and dolls) were readily available to support those activities. Sixth, by experimenting with other communicative strategies prior to using Icelandic, the children created an environment in which experimentation was the norm. This allowed Kelli to freely and comfortably assess and adjust her use of the language as a natural part of their play.

Recognising these conditions as supportive and taking into account the differences among children and their new cultural experiences, implications can be considered in terms of classroom environments. Specifically, Kelli's experiences urge teachers to consider the development of educational programmes in which:

- Second-language students have regular, frequent and prolonged opportunities to interact with native-speaking peers in the contexts of activities that are perceived *by the students* to be meaningful, rewarding, enjoyable and manageable.
- Students feel comfortable and confident enough to attempt participation and to use language.
- Materials and resources are readily available to encourage and facilitate interaction.

This means providing opportunities for frequent, comfortable, purposeful interaction not only in terms of informal associations among peers but with respect to the exploration of subject matter, transforming academic language use from what is often 'context-reduced' to that which is meaningfully 'context-embedded' (Cummins, 1980). Thought-provoking examples of second-language students and native-speakers investigating subject matter in meaningful, interactive contexts include Barry Taylor's (1987) description of 'real communication' in the multilingual classroom, Kathyrn Au's (1993) suggestions for creating classrooms as communities, Josie Levine's (1990) discussion of interactive environments, and Burgess and Gore's (1990) emphasis on collaborative, mixed-ability grouping. As these educators demonstrate, recognising the impact of peer interaction on second-language acquisition, and understanding the conditions which must exist in order for learning to take place, prompt careful and creative thought about an exciting range of pedagogical possibilities. The subsequent construction of educational programmes and development of supportive classroom environments have the potential to contribute significantly to students' understanding of language and life in the new culture in which they are attempting to get along.

References

Au, K. H. (1993) *Literacy Instruction in Multicultural Settings.* Orlando, Florida: Harcourt, Brave, Jovanovich College Publishers.

Bruner, J. (1983) *Child's Talk: Learning to use language.* New York: W. W. Norton.

Burgess, A. and Gore, L. (1990) 'The move from withdrawal ESL teaching to mainstream activities is necessary, possible and worthwhile', in J. Levine (Ed.), *Bilingual Learning and the Mainstream Curriculum.* London: Falmer Press.

Cummins, J. (1980) 'The construct of language proficiency in bilingual education', in Alatis, J. E. (Ed.) *Current Issues in Bilingual Education.* Washington, D.C: Georgetown University Press.

Ellis, R. (1985) *Understanding Second Language Acquisition.* Oxford: Oxford University Press.

Genishi, C. (1989) 'Observing Second Language Learning: An example of teachers learning', *Language Arts,* **66**(5), 509–15.

Hakuta, K. (1986) *Mirror of Language: The debate on bilingualism.* New York: Basic Books.

Hester, H. (1984) 'Peer interaction in learning English as a second language', *Theory into Practice* **23**(3), 208–17.

Huang, J. and Hatch, E. (1978) 'A Chinese Child's Acquisition of English', in E. M. Hatch (Ed.), *Second Language Acquisition: A book of readings.* Rowley, Mass: Newbury House.

Levine, J. (1990) *Bilingual learners and the Mainstream Curriculum.* London: Falmer Press.

Long, M. H. (1987) 'Native-speaker/non-native speaker conversation in the second language classroom', in Long, M. H. and Richard, J. C. (Eds) *Methodology in TESOL: A book of readings.* Boston: Heinle & Heinle Publishers.

Rigg, P. and Allen, V. G. (1989) *When They don't all Speak English: Integrating the ESL student into the regular classroom.* Urbana, Illinois: National Council of Teachers of English.

Taylor, B. P. (1987) 'Teaching ESL: Incorporating a communicative, student-centered component', in Long, M. H. and Richard, J. C. (Eds), *Methodology in TESOL: A book of readings.* Boston: Heinle & Heinle Publishers.

Wells, G. (1986) *The meaning makers: Children learning language and using language to learn.* Portsmouth, New Hampshire: Heinemann.

Wertsch, J. V. (1985) *Vygotsky and the Social Formation of Mind.* Cambridge, Mass: Harvard University Press.

Wong-Fillmore, L. (1986) 'Research Currents: Equity or excellence?', *Language Arts*, **63**(5), 474–81.
Wong-Fillmore, L. (1976) *The Second Time Around: Cognitive and social strategies in second language acquisition.* Unpublished doctoral dissertation, Stanford University.

Chapter 10

Working in partnership: parents, teacher and support teacher together

Maureen Turner

'What you think? I *am* better.' Rameen, at six years old, already sees herself as a successful learner of a second language. This unprompted evaluation of her progress formed part of a written dialogue with her much-loved teacher, towards the end of the summer term in year one, her second year in primary school.

Rameen had come to England two and a half years earlier at the age of four with her parents and her brother who is four years older. They lived at first in the south-east. Rameen went to nursery school in a new world – which looked, smelled and tasted quite different from her pleasant familiar life in Pakistan, with its elegant white houses, constant contact with family and friends, and endless blue skies. Overwhelmed by the strangeness of her new life, and struggling to communicate in a new language, she did not enjoy her first few months. Tears and unwillingness to go to school signalled her difficulty in coming to terms with a new language and culture.

The family then moved to Southampton where she joined the reception class of a primary school of approximately 300 children in the middle of an estate of mainly rented housing. This time the new class did not seem so strange, and she settled down to enjoying the activities and socialising. Her 'playground' vocabulary increased rapidly, and she made at least one good friend. However, as her English vocabulary increased, and with no opportunity to speak and develop her own language, she spoke less in Urdu, even to her parents. She frequently spent whole evenings speaking English with her best friend, and was beginning to turn her back on her first language. At this stage Rameen moved up to year one, and our paths crossed for the first time.

Beginning school – the first days

I had been visiting the school as a peripatetic teacher, part of the Section
11 provision for bilingual children in Southampton. Rameen's new class
teacher was concerned about the needs of bilingual children and, feeling
that she would like more information about meeting those needs most
effectively, had enrolled on the Hampshire course for classroom teachers,
funded by the Grants for Education Support and Training 16 (the British
Government's initiative for training mainstream teachers of bilingual
children). The course, called 'Teaching English across the Curriculum in
Multilingual Schools', was competency based and each course member
was supported by a tutor. As I was acting as tutor we decided to work
together for one morning a week.

Rameen was her only bilingual child, although elsewhere in the school
there were six others, joined during the year by three Vietnamese children.
None of the other children spoke Urdu. Rameen was doubly isolated: the
only child in her class whose mother tongue was not English, and the only
Urdu speaker in the infant school – her older brother was on the top floor
of the adjoining junior school and not accessible during the day. It would
have been useful to give her some time with a bilingual assistant but, as
she was not a beginner in English and was able to join in with classroom
activities, we could not spare our only Urdu speaker, who also works with
Farsi- and Panjabi-speaking children. As an isolated child Rameen clearly
needed language and cultural support. We asked her mother to join us for
a discussion about her progress, resulting in a two-way flow of
information about teaching and learning as Rameen was experiencing it.
(I did not bring an interpreter as I would normally do for a parental
conference because Rameen's mother speaks English well.)

Rameen's mother and class teacher already had a good relationship, and
we quickly sorted out practical points such as diet and absences for
festivals or extended visits home, some of the list of topics contained in
our parental conferencing form. We talked about the language spoken at
home, and the importance of continuing to develop Rameen's first
language. Rameen's mother was already sharing books with her in both
Urdu and English. Rameen had had some dual-language books in the
nursery and they both enjoyed using them. Rameem's mother was pleased
to be reassured that Rameen was not going to be confused by speaking
Urdu; she had felt that it was sad, but inevitable, that Urdu would be
eroded by the dominant 'school' language. She was interested to hear that
it would be useful to talk about number work and class topics in Urdu, to
help Rameen to sort out her ideas in her stronger language. She said she

would consider taking Rameen to Urdu classes later on when her English was more fluent. She agreed to join in with the 'parents book sharing' that happens at the beginning of most days in the infant classrooms in the school, where mums or dads can be found at the beginning of the morning sitting with their own child and one or two others enjoying a favourite story from the class book box. After the meeting the class teacher and I discussed our assessment of Rameem.

- She had been using English for two to three years and was conversationally fluent.
- She had friends and related well to a small group of girls.
- She had begun to read and write.
- She was performing within normal range for a year one child.
- She was quiet and self-contained for much of the time.

In view of needs elsewhere in the school, Rameen could have been considered as 'coping' in the classroom. We felt, however, that with extra effort and the application of research-based knowledge on our part she could do more than cope.

Adding a second language – or losing the first?

From our joint observation of Rameen and the background information from her mother, we felt that she had come into English before she had fully sorted out early concepts in her mother tongue. There has been much interest in recent years about the effect of the age of entry into a second language. Cummins (1984) argues strongly that second-language learning will be more effective if a child's mother tongue is well developed. When the first language is less secure, and when a child is immersed in a second language every day at school with a corresponding lack of incentive to develop home language, the learning of, and in, the second language may be impaired.

As she was only four when she came to England Rameen had still been exploring her world – making sense of new ideas, making connections, finding out about number, size, shape and the world of print. Pauline Gibbons (1991:6), writing about her work in Australia with children who have English as an additional language explains this in practical terms:

> So, if you have sorted out the world in one language, it becomes much easier to sort it out again in a second language. Children who arrive in school with a strong command of their first language and a developed range of concepts in that language are thus in a very favourable

position to learn English. They are adding on a second language to the one they already have (in much of the literature in the area they are referred to as 'additive bilinguals'). Younger children, whose language skills are less well developed, are in a less favourable position to learn a second language. With less conceptual and linguistic development, they have fewer pegs on which to hang new learning. It would seem that one of the worst times to switch language environments is around the age of five or six, when the comparative fragility of the first language does not support the learning of a second.

Rameen began to acquire English at the age of four and at six was continuing to become a fluent communicator in her second language. She was, therefore, switching language environments at a particularly difficult time. Gibbons goes on to stress that the first language should ideally continue to develop as the medium in which learning experiences take place. With this as a firm base there is no reason why fluency in other languages cannot be successfully acquired. However, so often the first language atrophies with lack of use as the new language takes over. This is increasingly likely to happen when the second language is seen as politically dominant. The danger here is that children can be left with neither language adequately developed for internalising new concepts. They may find it difficult to take on new vocabulary and structures needed for learning in the wider areas of the curriculum. It is, therefore, extremely important to provide support for developing the mother tongue wherever possible. Pauline Gibbons' observation that mother tongue is gradually replaced by English where bilingual children have little first language support gives weight to the belief of Rameen's mother that her use of Urdu would soon be eroded by English. If this happened, and neither language was adequately developed for learning, her progress in school could be impeded. It seemed, then, that without mother tongue support in school, and with fewer 'pegs' on which to hang each new idea, Rameen could be treading water rather than making progress.

Parent partnership

Ideally, we would have liked to give Rameem the opportunity to explore new concepts and discuss classroom tasks with our Urdu-speaking bilingual assistant, whose professional training and experience, linked with knowledge of immigrant children's mother tongue and culture, would have been a valuable resource for her. But Section 11 funding in

Hampshire (as elsewhere) is very thinly spread, and other commitments made it impossible to fit Rameen into her timetable.

However, Rameen's mother willingly became involved, not only in the morning booksharing but in writing a 'welcome' sign in Urdu on the door, visiting her son's class to talk about Eid and answer questions about Pakistan, and teaching Rameen's class to answer the register in Urdu. Rameen's confidence grew visibly during the year, and in the summer term she added Urdu 'emergent writing' to long written dialogues which she enjoyed producing. She considered it 'all right' for the class to use Urdu, but she did not want to teach words to them. When her teacher asked her why she would not, she said 'I don't want people to hear, only those who know my language.' Perhaps children learn to be quiet because they are unwilling to speak their first language and have not yet learned enough English to join in with the classroom chat. Often bilingual children are described as 'no trouble at all, they're so quiet'.

Rameen was certainly a quiet girl. She was included in a group of other 'quiet children' for a 15-minute session several times a week, led by an excellent special needs assistant who used a variety of stimuli to get conversation started. This was part of the flexible groupings for set purposes which the class teacher set up throughout the year. I sat in on two sessions and felt that, though Rameen was contributing to the discussion, she needed fluent language models so that she could hear and copy more varied structures.

'Modelling' by fluent language users during play and collaborative learning tasks is a natural way into a new language for children. Where a game or a task requires each child in the group to make contributions, good language learning is likely to take place.

We decided to make use of the hospital area already set up in the corridor bay. With notices saying 'X-ray', 'ward' and reception desk', and beds, cots and drawers full of bandages, it was an ideal place for role play, guaranteed to fascinate the chatty group of girls we chose to spend some time there with Rameen. The conversation was fragmented, with more 'playing alongside' than collaborative activity, but Rameen entered into the game with enthusiasm. The context was familiar to her, as she had visited an aunt in hospital to whom she refers at the end of the extract.

> *Rameem:* I know what the police number is – 999. The doctor is asking someone if they're a patient, and someone comes in.
>
> *Linda:* Let's put it over there
>
> *Susan:* Can I use the cooker?

Rameen: Look I've found a sticker.
Kate: I'm going to ring my real mum.
Susan: If you do the cooking you can wear this.
Raeem: I'm putting some clothes on this one [baby doll].
            [Finds a 'please be seated' notice.]
            I put this on the table. This can be the waiting room.
            [Later]
            We are mums but we have jobs in the hospital.
            We look after our own babies. She's going to have a hair wash [baby doll].
Susan: She's a newborn baby
Linda: Are you a patient?
Rameen: Yes.
Linda: What's wrong with you – a tummy ache?
Rameen: No – you know the muscles [shows arm] the muscles aren't very good. My auntie – we went to see my auntie the other day – she showed us the muscles in her arm – all blue and pink – the muscles weren't good.

From the talk generated in this role play we were able to see that Rameen would communicate more freely in friendship groups and where the context was familiar. After this she worked with a group of 'good talkers' who would model language which she could then use. For example, during a topic on 'waste and recycling', the class teacher sat with her group, and using 'concrete' objects which were familiar to Rameen in home context – milk cartons, crisp packets, chicken tikka sandwich wrappers – the teacher helped all the children discuss how packaging and other rubbish is generated at home, and what happens to it. During the discussion Rameen was absorbing the vocabulary and structures needed and was able to use the topic language herself. This was important. The opportunity to use specific language in context, rather than merely hear it, seems to be a vital and integral part of the learning process. Rameen was fired with enthusiasm by this topic and discussed it at home in Urdu with her mother.

Coping or achieving – mapping Rameen's language

We were now clear that Rameen was 'coping' with the curriculum, but we were not sure that she was even yet working at the level which she was potentially capable of achieving.

As part of the ongoing work on storytelling, Rameen's group produced a group picture book for the story *Not Now Bernard,* having first discussed which pictures each would contribute. While each child drew her allotted share, I asked her to tell me the story so that I could write it down (this method of assessment is mentioned in the excellent publication from the Birmingham Section 11 Project *A Language Map*). The focus of this assessment was to compare Rameen's ability to produce story-telling language with that of a cross section of other children in the class (all monolingual), and to pinpoint areas for development.

Linda's story

The monster bit Bernard's father and Bernard's father went purple and then he went 'Ow! Who bit me?' He went 'me' and then he said to the monster 'don't bite me'. And he went to see Bernard's mother and she said 'do you want a drink Bernard? 'Yes' said the monster and once he drunk it he said 'but I'm a monster!' Bernard's mother said 'I can't be bothered, just go up to bed.'

Sarah's story

He annoyed his dad. He hurt his finger. He's gone green. His mum said, 'not now Bernard'. He said, 'a monster's in the garden'. He ate Bernard up. The monster went inside the house. His mum thinked it was Bernard and his dad thinked it was Bernard. The monster bit dad. Mum watered the plants. She said Bernard's tea was ready. The monster goes to bed then he said he was a monster.

Rameen's story

Mum said 'not now Bernard'. She was getting a drink of water. When the dad was doing something busy Bernard disturbed dad. Then dad hit his finger. Then his face got blue. I liked the bit where the monster's behind her. Bernard went in the back garden and said, 'hello monster' then he ate him, then he went inside. He said, 'roar'. Mother said, 'not now Bernard'. The monster was behind her. The monster bite dad's leg then Dad screamed. His face got purple. Then Bernard's mum called Bernard. 'Your dinner's ready Bernard.' The monster came and ate it, then he watched telly. The monster was reading one of Bernard's comics and broke one of Bernard's toys. Well, the monster hat (*sic*) to go to bed and mother said 'your milk is upstairs'. The monster said 'I don't want to go to bed.'

Cathy's story (part)

Watering plants. Bernard said. 'hallo'. The father said, 'not now Bernard'. He hit his finger. Mum was getting some water. The water's come out.

Rameen's lively re-telling of the story was further evidence of her love of books and reading. She employed several interesting words such as 'busy' 'disturbed' and 'screamed' not used by the others, which showed that she was acquiring a wide vocabulary. The indications of second-language acquisition came in problems with handling idiom: 'he got purple' and 'his face got blue'. The story was dictated in November, but her difficulty with this idiomatic usage was echoed when she was making a get-well card for a sick classmate in the summer term: 'I hope you get happy from this letter', and in her cheerful self-evaluation at the opening of this chapter.

The strategy of working in a group of children who are using language competently and freely, on which her class teacher and I had already agreed, would help her to become confident in handling idiomatic use of auxiliary verbs as she moved through year one into year two.

The fluency trap

We were however concerned that her written work was not keeping pace with her oral skills. It was clear that she was an able child, capable of performing at what is considered to be the average National Curriculum level in English for her age although working in her second language; but the present level of her control of the new language was more apparent when she was writing. This was an activity which she pursued enthusiastically, often repeating herself and increasing the size of her letters so that she could fill up a page. The extra effort of communicating through writing threw up areas of syntax and idiom where she was less secure. This pattern is common among children speaking a second language, who may be caught in a 'fluency trap' when conversational fluency outstrips the acquisition of literacy skills, often leading to a mistaken concern that a pupil may have special educational needs.

As part of the work for her course Rameen's class teacher was examining the provision in school for bilingual pupils. There has existed in the past in many British schools confusion between the needs of children whose mother tongue is not English, and those of children considered to have special educational needs. This had been addressed over a period in school through discussion with staff using the assessment of a group of pupils as a focus. Deryn Hall's excellent book *Living in Two Languages* (1995) was useful in clarifying issues and procedures for separating out the needs of the two groups and charting a course of action for individual pupils.

We recognised, however, that the introduction of individual education plans for special educational needs pupils in the wake of the 1994 Code of Practice was useful in focusing on the next stage of the pupil's development and strategies for achieving success.

My colleague felt that this could also be a useful tool for bilingual pupils, and one which she could use to focus on Rameen's writing, if she could devise a format which clearly differentiated the two groups. She realised, however, that it was important to preserve the hard-won distinction laid down in the 1981 Education Act that bilingualism does not, in itself, constitute a 'special need'. Teachers of English as an additional language have fought hard over the years to clarify the difference between the small-step, over-learning approach which benefits many special educational needs pupils, and the need of bilingual pupils for wide experience of language in the classroom environment fostered by collaborative working on challenging tasks with able pupils.

She decided to produce an alternative individual educational plan format which could be used in school with bilingual children. The purpose of this would be to help class teachers formulate the next stage of development of their bilingual pupils. An important feature was that an entry had to be made stating the length of time a child had been learning English, which is surprisingly often overlooked when a bilingual child is being discussed.

The individual education plan which was formulated for Rameen at the beginning of the summer term set targets and success criteria which focused directly on the writing.

Targets	*Success criteria*
To improve handwriting.	Form all letters correctly.
To begin to join letters.	Learn and write simple joining patterns.
To learn more sight words.	To read sight words for next reading level.
To improve spelling.	Learn 10 new spellings and use in writing.
To structure a story.	Write a story with a beginning, middle and end.

Rameen and her mother were involved in a discussion of the targets, and also the review at the end of the term. Her mother was able to support and encourage Rameen's writing at home, in addition to sharing books with her, which they both enjoyed enormously.

By the end of the summer term, Rameen's writing was becoming more structured and she, herself, was conscious that she was now more successful. Rameen's class teacher, evaluating her progress at the end of the year, concluded that the most significant improvements had been in reading and writing.

Conclusion

Teacher, child and parent working together

Rameen's progress during the year was good. She gained a full year of reading age over a few months, and her writing improved to her satisfaction. This was important for her self-esteem, a vital component of successful learning. Her confusion at times during mathematics groups alerted us to the continuing need to check that she understood concepts at each step, and the importance of working on tasks in a small group where she could test her ideas and ask questions, rather than relying exclusively on the 'try and think' method in isolation.

The components of Rameem's success

Her own individual strengths were her skill as a language learner, her enthusiasm and her security in the support of her parents for the learning process. This was maximised by the partnership between Rameen's mother and her class teacher, with the support of the specialist peripatetic teacher. The parents' strengths – their prior knowledge of their daughter and her development, their own enjoyment of books and their high expectations of her – were recognised and built on by the class teacher who was able to draw them into the life of the school. Consequently, the potential weaknesses of their position – uncertainty about the British education system and shyness in approaching their school – were offset by becoming part of the school community.

The partner who was most directly concerned with Rameen during the day was her class teacher. Her friendliness and sympathy were vital in establishing a working relationship, as was her commitment to the quality of her pupil's learning.

Equally important, perhaps, was her realisation that she did not know how to get the best for her bilingual pupil and her willingness to undertake a demanding course over two terms to find out. The course, which was offered to all mainstream teachers in Hampshire, proved valuable not only by contributing to the professional development of teachers who undertook it, but also by providing their schools with the opportunity to examine resources and school policies for bilingual children. The course not only addressed the class teacher's need for specific information, but also mitigated that overwhelming difficulty encountered by any class teacher – lack of time. Specific knowledge of strategies and cultural information gained from the course meant that provision for bilingual learners could be quickly slotted in at each stage of long-, medium- and short-term planning in the school, and in individual classrooms.

Though the contribution to a partnership of the specialist peripatetic teacher is necessarily less than the class teacher's and of shorter duration, the combination of experience and access to information and research, which is offered by specialist teachers, plays a major part in the education of bilingual pupils throughout the country, both directly and through influence on school, local education authority and national policies. Their more recent role as providers of training for mainstream teachers is likely to have an increasingly important effect. The contribution of bilingual assistants also, where they are available, is of crucial importance to happiness and successful learning.

As I evaluated what I had learned from the process, I became more convinced of the need to support children beyond the initial stages of acquiring English. Mills and Mills (1993) suggests that learning through a second language is always less efficient until the child has been working in the language for four years. Jim Cummins (1984) talked of the need for five to seven years' experience in a language before all subjects of the curriculum can fully accessed. This view is taken by other researchers, and was reiterated by him in an address at Reading University in April 1996. For Rameen there is a long way to go before she is learning on the same terms as her classmates. Without support through Urdu in school she has been working with at least one hand tied behind her back. The dangers of this for the development of cognition in young children have been frequently stressed (Gibbons, 1991:61):

> Most kindergarten children who enter school with little or no English are, by necessity, expected to learn within the confines of a very limited range of language – their current level of development in English. These children have full capacity for learning, but in an English-only class they are without the language which will allow them to do so. In this situation their cognitive and conceptual development may be slowed down or hampered while they are acquiring sufficient fluency in English.

Fortunately the partnership of family and school in this case has helped the child through this difficult period and, hopefully, will continue to do so right through her school career. We need, therefore, to foster continuing partnerships of parents, support teachers and class teachers who have access to specific training; and we need to ensure that the pupils themselves have the motivation and self-esteem that comes from encouragement by sympathetic and knowledgeable schools. If we can achieve these goals we are more likely to be able to give all bilingual pupils a fair chance of achieving the best possible outcome from their education.

References

Baker, C. (1993) *Foundations of Bilingual Education and Bilingualism.* Clevedon: Multilingual Matters.

Cummins, J. (1984) *Bilingualism and Special Education: Issues in assessment and pedagogy.* Clevedon: Multilingual Matters.

Cummins, J. (1996) Address at Reading University, April 1996.

Education Act 1981. Department of Education and Science. London: HMSO.

Gibbons, P. (1991) *Learning to Learn in a Second Language.* Newtown: Primary English Teaching Association, Australia.

Hall, D. (1995) *Assessing the Needs of Bilingual Pupils – Living in two languages.* London: Fulton.

Hampshire Bilingual Learners Support Service (1995) *Guidelines.*

Mills, J. and Mills, R. (1993) *Bilingualism in the Primary School.* London: Routledge.

Tweedle, J. and Simpson, M. (1995) *A Language Map.* Section 11 Project: Birmingham.

Chapter 11

Why you don't eat bananas: an exploration of a child's possible worlds in story

Inge Cramer

> I maded before that ages ago story   and then that film came on   and
> I said *yes*   that film came on   then I been dancing about *table
> and been close the little girl's door so other people can't see me   and
> I closened the curtain on my door so then I keep on   my mother said
> *what's happening to you*   she said it's *not which film that which you
> put on and made up that story*   and I saided *no this is that other one*
> and then she said *OK that one*   then she joined me   then my dad
> came   and I said *it's a film which I maded* that new one   and he
> started to dance with me us lot   *oh my god* and my cousin came
> they started laughing   and I changed my clothes   it was my dancing
> where they dance in the shows   and I was dancing with my cousin[1]

This story indicates, I hope, even in its edited, transcribed and therefore
flattened form, the excitement to be generated for a child by oral
storymaking. 'That film' referred to a video Zohra had just retold in story
form and, although she was aware of the distinction between true and
invented stories, she seems here almost to view herself as its inventor.
Zohra speaks increasingly rapidly, half-laughing and half-shouting as she
relates what her mother said. She displays her awareness of appropriate
cultural contexts by mentioning that she had closed the curtains so that
people outside the family should not see her. Watching mainly Hindi
videos seems to be an extended family experience involving, in this case,
both parents and cousins.

1 Extra space has been inserted to separate sense units. See the key on page 160 for an
   explanation of the symbols used in these transcriptions. I would like to express my
   thanks to Kalsoom Bibi and Rashda Mohammed for the translation of Panjabi words.

Oral storymaking offers a child immense possibilities to become a significant meaning-maker. It does so all the more powerfully because it intertwines cognition with affect. Yet, because many children seem to tell stories so readily in their early years, we may not always value the activity in school. A casual listener may pay too great attention to Zohra's developing but, as yet, imperfect control of English syntax without appreciating that, as she invents or retells often long and complex plots with many characters, she is exploring all kinds of discourses and themes. However, it is crucial for teachers to understand children like Zohra's first steps into story-telling if they are to facilitate their learning of a new language in school. In this chapter I shall first look at ways in which Zohra begins to enter a new world using story telling as a mediator, and then go on to examine implications for teachers working in multilingual classrooms.

Getting to know Zohra

Zohra is a bilingual six-year-old child growing up in a city in the north of England. Her family originates from the Mirpur district of Pakistan. She speaks Panjabi with her grandmother, a mixture of Panjabi and English with both of her parents, and English with her cousins and aunties. She is a Muslim and attends a multi-ethnic primary school. Most children at the school are of south-Asian origin as were, at the time of this study, most of the teachers in reception, year one and year two. English, however, is the dominant language of the school. National Curriculum English, within which Zohra's teacher must work, barely recognises the cultures and lives of those who do not belong to England's ethnic majority; nor do many educational resources commercially available. Yet numerous research studies (Skutnabb-Kangas, 1988; Gregory, 1996) stress the advantages of recognising bilingual education and cultural difference. A collection of the children's *own* stories is likely to be one of the teacher's most important resources, as we shall see below.

Zohra was one of a group of six children in the school who worked with me on 14 occasions during the school year. The children usually told their stories in pairs, sometimes single-sex, sometimes girl-boy. To record the stories clearly enough for accurate transcription, I had to abandon working in the classroom. The children were free to refuse to come, and they could refuse to tell a story. This rarely happened. They could listen to themselves on the tape recorder, and I would give them a typescript of at least one of their stories on my next visit. The procedure for eliciting the stories varied; I would usually ask if they had a story to tell me first, saying that I would really like to hear one they might have invented or heard at home. I would sometimes tell or read a story either before or after they had told one. There were optional picture prompts on two occasions. Sometimes they drew; sometimes I would write. Zohra decided that oral storytelling was 'really gorgeous'.

Zohra's stories

Zohra told at least 22 longer stories during the year, which I categorised roughly into likely predominant sources: personal, book, video and invented. It is not easy to do this (Fox, 1993:15–20): most stories have a variety of sources and it is important that retelling itself is considered as a form of invention.

Almost all the stories told had some verbal audience feedback by either the storytelling partner or myself, as the following excerpt from the transcript of *Cinderella Rose Princess* shows. On this occasion there were many more interruptions than usual, partly because I repeated Zohra's words as I wrote, and partly because Zohra was language-switching. We see below how she begins to explain to me the meaning of a Panjabi word, transliterated as 'bolah'.

Teacher:	who said . mum . Rama's mum
Zohra:	yeah . Rama's mum . ^ (1.0) said . that (3.0) he don't know . erm . everyone says that he don't know anything . he's a . soft and he's a bolah and he . don't
Teacher:	he's a soft what
Zohra:	he's a soft kind of bolah
Teacher:	what's a = bolah
Zohra:	= bolah means . bolah means that he's er
Rashid:	he got a balls . a ball
Zohra:	no . not . he's a soft . that's mean . soft means er . bolah
Teacher:	you mean he's stupid
Zohra:	he's a bolah . he's
Teacher:	stupid
Rashid:	soft
Zohra:	yeah . and he sings this song

This exchange between Zohra and myself underlines the importance of *bilingual* teachers: it takes me some time to establish what 'bolah' might mean and I never quite understand that Zohra's use of the word 'soft' is more appropriate than my 'stupid'. She does not mean that Rama is stupid; rather, that he is innocent or naive. Interruptions like this or the following

Teacher:	why can't she [go outside]
Zohra:	'cos er . she not allowed

may well have influenced the course of the story. Zohra's stories, therefore, are not entirely her independent constructions. I usually tried not to intervene too much, although audience response is itself a part of the story-telling process. Moreover, provided it is not disruptive to the flow, genuine puzzlement may well be helpful, for it indicates a need for clarification.

Cinderella Rose Princess: the power of videos

Transcription is an uncertain business. It is not always easy to understand what a child is saying. In *Cinderella Rose Princess,* Zohra's pronunciation of 'prince' or 'princess' sounded virtually identical to 'twins'; she told stories about all three, but the text suggests 'princess'. The removal of garbles and interchanges is also problematic, as is the lack of prosodic information. The edited form offered, however, should allow the reader some holistic sense of the stories.

When Zohra announced her title, I was expecting a story with whose broad outline I might be familiar because of the name 'Cinderella Rose'. On two previous occasions she had retold the Disney *Snow White* and the central character had been called 'Rose'. Instead, and to my delight, she retold the video, mentioned in the opening story, *Annari.*

first Cinderella princess goes outside   the man comes riding cycle a king's son   and he has in his hand a red umbrella   and when everyone sees red umbrella they runs away in they house   this monkey he lefts outside   and he gotted this mat on his face   and he said to *hide his face*   and this chotay rajah this little rajah he whoever looks or talk by his sister he will cut the heads all in half   and he will cut this half [of their moustache] and they hairs the sister had nother   sisters had a sahliay   sahliay means friend   she calls the sahliay to 'em   and she was skipping in the house   the sahliahns was coming to her to play with   they were laughing   and she said *hey you camed*   and they said that   *let's go and play outside*   she didn't give a answer back to her   she was really upset   she said that *who gonna take me outside   I can't*   then she said that *who's this*   and this little sahliay said that *this is my cousin   she just came today in this area   and why don't you play outside*   she said that *well I'm not allowed*   then Ragoo came Ragoo is his noker slave   she asked that *my sahliay's came   will you make some dinner*   she said that *go bring dinner   bring apple and a fruit* and that noker said that *OK I am coming now* the Cinderella changed** Cinderella's big birthday came and this Rama he went to sing a song and everyone thinks so he's a bolah   everyone thinks he don't know anything for the day Rama's mum said that *I know he gone in the khawayli*   khawayli means that it's a big house there   Rama's mum says that *he don't know anything   he's soft   and he's a bolah*   and he sings the song and he was saying   *choti zari piari nanni ai* [my small beloved has come]   it were a nice song *choti din nanni piari ai heh* [my little sweetheart has come]   that song is so gorgeous   I sing my head off   and he was singing   and he came back home at the night time   and his mother said *now what why you came now   you could have stayed there and eat the dinner from the khawayli   and you like in the khawayli dinner too much*   and he saided that *what you're saying I didn't even have no glass of water today*   and his mum said that *oh ≠ mummy you know what   khawayli dhey bunday itenay thaweez kurteh heh* [the people of the palace do magic to make someone love]   *they likes me too much the song that man burray rajah*   [the big rajah] they said that *he's nice a person songing   and he like a radio singing a song*   and he said that *mummy will you take a karna* [food] *out and make me eat with your hands dinner*   the mummy said that *you're so big and you're still eating from my hand   take it out for yourself and eat it by yourself* Rama said that *what what you said   you're not gonna make your hands to eat*   and he was starting to sing that song again *choti sahliay nemni piari heh* [the little sweetheart is coming]   *anay koy dhar nehin hotha* [there's no fear in coming]   and that's when he sanged and after that he's sleeping the mandar you know where you pray to God and he slept there   and his mum came   and she's got his dinner and his mum   came and said *Rama will you eat now*   he said *no I'm not   why did you say that you're not gonna make me eat like that mujhhe lachar mandar* [take me to the temple]   he's trying to sing that song after his dinner   the mummy's joined in   and then he gotted a job in the khawayli and then he said *to clean*   and Cinderella Rose princess said that *I'm so happy*   and he put her hand on his head   and the chotay rajah came   he saided that *you holded my sister's hand why did you put on sandukh [?] on his head*   and he saided that *sorry I'm not gonna do it again* and then they stopped smacking him   and then they started to laugh at him   and that's the end

Questioning afterwards showed that there was more to the plot: a plan to kill Cinderella involving electric shocks in factories, and a marriage between Cinderella and Rama.

What delighted me about this story? First, Zohra had, for only the second time in four months, told a story that clearly drew on experiences that were important to her in the context of home. After this she used such video material much more. The Indian setting is signalled by a variety of clues: the inclusion of a monkey in the opening orientation, Rama's name, and the allusions to 'rajah' and 'mandar'. Some of the dominant themes are characteristic of Hollywood films.

Second, she felt able to switch languages (see the example of 'bolah' above). She may have done so either because she was retelling a Hindi video or because Rashid was present. Writing, by encouraging a slower pace, gave me a chance to ask for translations, which she then seemed to provide almost automatically: *Zohra:* said that er . I know he gone in the . in the khawayli . khawayli means that it's a big house there. She knows how to use analogies, for in another story her central character says: 'I'm gonna make you like my house like a castle'. But here she used 'khawayli', akin to the English word 'mansion' or 'palace'. 'Sahliay' means 'friend'; more precisely, it means 'female friend' and it is her preferred term, perhaps because of its emotional and gender connotations.

Stories as significant discourses: independence and the family

The themes in *Cinderella Rose Princess* of restrictions on girls, of rich and poor, of conflict between mother and son, or of someone poor and scorned attaining success and status through music, are familiar to most children growing up in England. Zohra often focused on the contrast between poor and rich. Poor people might become rich, become 'queens' and 'kings'. The acquisition of wealth entails helping other people. Zohra's longest story, *Rose,* offers us a clear example. After hearing 'two horrible mans' call her names, Rose uses her father's money, despite his initial opposition, to give clothes, make new houses, provide education, work and entertainment for the people in her neighbourhood:

and she made some school for the childrens and a college and a [school name] and these all schools and she made for a old mans a library for a children library and she putten gas cooker like these food and all gas cookers and drawers every one things for a kitchen and she made a nice kitchen and dining tables she buyded for everyone and they all thing was same but she putted it in a different order which anys is best

Most of Zohra's thirteen video and invented stories centre strongly on the family. Children have obligations, they raise money for their family, but they also run away, disobey their parents, tease the cat, steal (and replace) money. I do not speculate why Zohra told particular stories or what, psychologically, they could have meant to her, but norms and values are clearly being articulated and questioned (Bearne, 1994:89–90). The stories provide evidence of some of the significant discourses through which Zohra is both being enculturated and exploring her sense of identity, however fictional a construct 'identity' may be. She is rehearsing the discourses of more powerful adults. She seems also to be 'trying out "what if..." kinds of experiences, especially those that are forbidden, dangerous, excessive or impossible in everyday life. Saying things doesn't make them happen' (Fox, 1993:196).

The following story, *Monkey in the Fair*, centres on relationships with family and friends, on wants, desires and their opposites. Zohra seems to play with problems of family, nurture and independence:

there was five monkey in the forest   there was a baby   the baby said *I don't like to stay in the forest   I want to stay in the fair*   and he runned off   and he runnded away from his mummy and his daddy and his sister   and he saw another little fair   and he wanted to have a ride on the swings   then he paid the monies   and he saw on the giraffe and he said *please could I sit on your back* and the giraffe   said *yes* and the giraffe he were reading a story to a monkey   and the monkey said *oh thank you*   and he runned off to a lion   then lion chased after the monkey   and monkey went on the fair   the monkey went on the swings   and you know where there bes a stick   and he jump   he went on the swings so higher   and he jumped on the stick   then the lion couldn't find him   and the lion went away   and the lion said that when the lion's little babies and he said *sorry I couldn't find you a monkey   I finded one and I don't know where he went*   then the babies runned   the baby crieded   and they said that *I'm not gonna to play for you   I'm never gonna should you catch you one monkey for me so we could eat him now   we're not gonna eat none monkeys we're just gonna be hungry every day gonna eat nothing* they said that *we're gonna be monkey's friend for ever* and they runned off and the monkey played with them they finded a monkey and they played with it they said that *I don't want to eat you look I'm sorry from my daddy he's really bad to me so I'm your friend right I'm not gonna eat nothing of monkeys and I'm just going to be hungry* and the monkey said that *oh no no don't be hungry why you don't eat bananas* the lion said *banana but I didn't tasted banana could I taste please the banana* and the monkey gave the banana and they said that *mmm they delicious they nice then we want some more please* and they moved they head and they sawded a cherries high up the trees even the strawberries and cherries they asked the monkey *we could see a strawberry and cherry please could you please get them for us on the tree* and the monkey went on the tree quickly and he bringed back loads of pair of strawberry and he went on the other tree and he gotted a cherries and they all ated it together they said that *oh leave them from the rest where we're gonna sleep* and the monkey said *oh I finded a little house let's see who's in there* there was a princess and they said that *let's go inside* they knocked on the door and princess inside came out and she say *oh you I like monkey even little kittens of lions* and she bringed them inside and she slept with them all that time and even morning time and they waked up and the princess said that *let's go sit on that big ride which had turns* and the monkey and the lion didn't they said *oh no no I don't want to sit on there* and the princess said *just try it bes too funny* and they sat on it and they tried it and they were laughing and laughing all the time even at the night time they gone off of it and the princess said *let's eat share out the sweets* even the monkey said *we got a cherries even a strawberries* and they shared it out and the lion gived the ring and monkey gived the necklace

The dialogue is as central to the plot as the action, for much of the 'action' takes place in dialogue. Dialogue also externalises a range of emotions: desire, apology, revulsion and denial. Although her control of English lexicogrammar is yet to be fully established, Zohra uses both analogy, 'little kittens of lions', and rhetoric effectively. The lion cubs, rejecting their father, use five emphatic declarations, four of them negative, one of which is heightened by a double negative; the positive 'we're just gonna be hungry every day' is sandwiched between two references to eating nothing. Time is emphasised by the use of 'never', 'every day' and 'for ever'.

The lions know they will be hungry as a consequence but the monkey presents them with a novel solution: become vegetarian. 'Why you don't eat bananas?' This conversation is a crucial point in the story. It is marked by expressive phonology, raised pitch and lengthened words like 'nice' and 'please'. Is it excessive to suggest that Zohra is creating her own 'possible worlds through the metaphoric transformation of the ordinary and the conventionally given' (Bruner, 1986:49)? As Chukovsky (1963:598) suggests, to be able to do this she has to be 'keenly aware of the normal'.

Inversions of 'normality' occur in many of Zohra's stories. Some squirrels hide a watermelon from their mother. The mice eat the watermelon so the squirrels eat the mice. When their father later shares another watermelon with them, their mother wakes up and asks what is happening. The squirrels say: *'mummy tomorrow daddy gotted a job daddy went in a work now ≠ this time at the night time . er . (...) yeah . there's some work bes opened.'*

Zohra is specific that it's a 'joke' on the mummy, although she also seems familiar with the concept of night shifts. Many stories later, she laughs at the idea that rich people turn into poor people and that

Zohra:	these nickers [burglars] came in . they are outside . they killded all the ladies (1.0) and then there's only man . to dance . and sing a song (2.0) 'cos er . you know the poor people . they likened the ladies' dance . dance heh . the (1.0)
Ferhana:	men
Zohra:	(2.0) rich people liked the ladies' dance . dance heh . so . the man have to dance like ladies (1.0) <laughs>

It is not uncommon for men to dance, but it amuses her when they have to dance like women.

In story telling, affect and logic work together (Meek, 1991:237) and they offer a powerful context both for learning a language and learning through language. Zohra is exploring her possible worlds. Be it through inversion, through causality and temporality or through listing the components of a neighbourhood fit to live in, she is organising and constructing categories and connections, and her stance towards them.

What teachers can learn from Zohra's stories: implications for classroom practice

The importance of affect and of play in language acquisition and development has often been stressed. Oral storytelling, however, remains largely neglected in schools, partly because of the difficulties of organisation, and partly, perhaps, because there is a fear that storytelling is not the stuff of which educational achievement is made. Storymaking is more likely to be associated with writing, with the accompanying limitations imposed by transcription. My small case study confirms that storytelling is cognitively demanding whilst simultaneously providing supportive contexts for language learning, if the person listening is accepting and approving (Sutton-Smith *et al*, 1981:30–5). Children acquiring another language may be presented with unnecessary difficulties at the age of six years and beyond because they are regarded as too old for play and yet too young for the use of overt cognitive or literacy strategies (John-Steiner, 1985:353–4).

Why is storymaking so powerful a support for language learning and cognitive development? It is because it operates on so many levels. It brings into operation the positive consequences of play and affect whilst using everyday schemas and familiar chunks of story language. It offers longer speaking turns than normal in classrooms and can shift topic initiation to the child. It conjoins oracy and literacy.

Children and their caregivers need to know that storymaking is a challenging and legitimate form of work. Children should hear and retell stories for themselves from a variety of texts, from video and from personal experience. Teachers need to check that they model stories that are relevant to children's lives, and that represent and celebrate the diversity of cultural experience with a variety of heroes and styles.

Whilst the notion of modelling on texts is helpful, the principles of invention and borrowing are also critical. Children need to become confident in knowing that they can create stories of their own, in whichever language or mix of languages they like, using bits from whatever source they like. Rather than only being given a particular story to retell, they should be asked which stories they might like to tell, which they get told at home and so on. A teacher is thereby more likely to give the child a chance of bringing all her cultures into the classroom, rather than simply replicating the almost inescapable dominant cultural messages offered by the choices of texts from publishers, one's own preferences and the social and institutional practices of school. If we write them down, we need to use the child's own language forms. Changes that are made can sometimes offer fruitful discussion points but, on the whole, responses should concentrate on the child's meanings rather than on rephrasing syntax. In responding to meaning, after all, the listener simultaneously models the conventional adult linguistic forms.

The management of oral storymaking in a busy classroom may be demanding but opportunities need to be provided. There are many helpful books and articles (for example, Howe and Johnson, 1992, or Shell, 1992). The most important points are listed below:

- Regular and frequent storytelling by adults and children.
- An acceptance of retelling.
- The encouragement of invention.
- Different audiences and group sizes.
- Storytelling in all available languages.
- Collaborative as well as individual storymaking.
- The regular use of the tape recorder so children can listen to themselves.
- A variety of prompts to cater for individual learning styles, but with a stress on 'is there any story you would like to make up or tell?'
- A variety of collection styles, from spontaneous to described.

Zohra presents a further compelling case. It is particularly useful to collect a corpus of stories and to try to analyse what the child is doing, relating this also to our responses and to the kinds of story we customarily offer. After a while Zohra drew freely on all the cultures she had access to for material with which to construct her stories. Not all the children in my study did so as clearly. The encouragement to tell stories based on videos helped in this. She never, however, gave her female heroes south-Asian names. Given the dominance of Anglo-American culture in the media and the printed word, I needed to make the presence of children from minority cultures much more visible in the ways I used my stories. The mere inclusion of stories like *Sinbad the Sailor or Mr Hussain and the Trousers* was not enough.

There is little research on telling stories in mother tongue (Morrison and Sandhu, 1992:102 and Blackledge, 1993:134). We know that language and cultural identity are intimately linked, that without bilingual education Zohra's linguistic development in both her languages is under threat. We need to understand her mother tongue for her to be able to use her metaphors, her language awareness, her comparisons and draw upon her experiences effectively. Though young, she already knows about the dangers of language loss:

> there's one true story   and this I'm telling you now   (...)   do you know this girl   she was right stupid   these nickers they made her like stupid   and she kept on saying that to her mum *oh my mum keep on saying this and that I'm stupid*   and she's keep on laughing   then she says again *ohhhh my mum told that I'm stupid I'm not*   she was a Muslim girl   and now she don't know her language

Surely our ultimate aim should be to enable Zohra to draw on all the cultures to which she has access, and to feel at home in using both her languages in school.

Key to transcripts

.	micropause
(2.0)	number of seconds in a pause
^	back channel (mhmh, mmm etc.)
[]	translations of Panjabi or
	additions to help indicate meaning
(…)	omission of T-Unit(s)
=	beginning of overlapping speech
*	unclear syllable
italics	dialogue in the story
≠	inferred change of speaker; no tag
<laughs>	non-verbal behaviour

References

Bearne, E. (1994) 'Where Do Stories Come From?', in Styles, M., Bearne, E. and Watson, V. (Eds) *The Prose and the Passion: Children and their reading*. London: Cassell.

Blackledge, A. (1993) 'We Can't Tell Our Stories in English': Language, story and culture in the primary school', *Language, Culture and Curriculum*, 6 (2), 130–41.

Bruner, J. S. (1986) *Actual Minds, Possible Worlds*. Cambridge, Mass: Harvard University Press.

Chukovsky, K. (1963) 'The Sense of Nonsense Verse', in Bruner, J. S., Jolly, A. and Sylva, K. (1976). *Play: Its role in development and evolution*. Harmondsworth: Penguin.

Fox, C. (1993) *At the Very Edge of the Forest: The influence of literature on storytelling by children*. London: Cassell.

Gregory, E. (1996) *Making Sense of a New World: Learning to read in a second language*. London: Paul Chapman Publishing.

Howe, A. and Johnson, J. (1992) *Common Bonds: Storytelling in the classroom*. London: Hodder & Stoughton.

John-Steiner, V. (1985) 'The road to Competence in an Alien Land: A Vygotskian perspective on bilingualism' in Wertsch, J. V. (Ed.) *Culture, Communication, and Cognition: Vygotskian perspectives*. Cambridge: Cambridge University Press.

Meek, M. (1991) *On Being Literate*. London: The Bodley Head.

Morrison, M. and Sandhu, P. (1992) 'Towards a Multilingual Pedagogy', in Norman, K. (Ed.) *Thinking Voices: The work of the National Oracy Project*. London: Hodder & Stoughton.

Shell, R (compiler) (1992) *Language Works*. Tower Hamlets, London: Learning by Design.

Skutnabb-Kangas, T. (1988) 'Multilingualism and the Education of Minority Children', in Skutnabb-Kangas, T. and Cummins, J. (Eds) *Minority Education: From shame to struggle*. Clevedon: Multilingual Matters Ltd.

Sutton-Smith, B. in collaboration with Abrams, D. M., Botvin, G. J., Caring, M-L., Gildesgame, D. P., Mahony, D. H. and Stevens, T. R. (1981) *The Folk Tales of Children*. Publications of the American Folklore Society, New Series, Vol. 3. Philadelphia: University of Pennsylvania Press.

Children's books

Walker, B. K. (1989) *Turkish Folktales for Children, Vol. 4.* Atatürk Culture Centre Publication No. 30: Ankara.
Williams, M. (1994) *Sinbad the Sailor.* London: Walker Books.

Chapter 12

From Karelia to Kashmir: a journey into bilingual children's story-reading experiences within school and community literacy practice

Leena Robertson

From Karelia to Kashmir

Forests have many names in Finnish. When I was little I learnt these names through stories. My grandmother would spin tales of trolls, spirits and fairies that lived in Finland's deepest and greenest pine forests as effortlessly as I could listen, and my grandfather would tell endless, amazingly accurate, but hilariously funny stories of real people of real Karelia, where my maternal family had always lived, and where we belonged – but where I had never been. In my mind Karelia had the prettiest of waters, funniest of people and most mysterious of forests. Karelia, a substantial part of Finland, had been lost to the Soviet Union during the Second World War and, in my childhood, the pain was still visible in the adults' eyes. For my fifth birthday my parents gave me a classic book of Finnish fairy tales written in the early 20th century. The author, Anni Swann, carried on the Finnish children's story tradition of teaching children to 'love thy God and thy land'. She combined her stories with Finnish folklore and an unyielding devotion to children, nature and animals. By setting the majority of her tales in the middle of the vast pine forests, they are firmly set in Finnish culture.

I have vivid as well as very hazy recollections of playing outside, and I remember how the real forests and trees around our home transformed themselves into the very same settings I had seen and heard in these stories. I named them according to the stories, and often asked my mother and my grandmother, as I trailed behind them on our berry picking rambles, 'Could that be the little fairies' grove? Could that be the glade where the forest trolls danced?' And my grandmother would nod her head, smile knowingly, and then begin to tell one of her stories. The oral stories of my grandparents gave me a firm sense of belonging, whereas the written fairy-tales, and their old-fashioned language and religious undertones, gave me a dawning sense of past. At the statutory age of seven I went to school, and learnt to read with my ABC book (Aapinen) which had pictures of forests and trolls, not very different to the ones I had become so closely acquainted with in Swann's tales. The countless other books and comics that I was subsequently given, and my readings of these, all carried some indefinable traces of Anni Swann's fairy tales with them, which in my mind had by then become hopelessly enmeshed with Karelia, its people and past.

Years later, I am teaching a mixed reception/year one class in the centre of Watford, an old-established market town some 20 miles north of London. I am the class teacher and the children in my class are four-to-six year olds who are predominantly emergent bilinguals (16 out of 26) and of Pakistani origin. About 5 per cent of Watford's population is from the areas of Azad Jammu and Kashmir in Pakistan, and particularly from Kashmir. The parents of these children were generally born in Pakistan, but most of the school's pupils (75 per cent of Pakistani origin) were born in Watford and have attended the school's nursery. At home they speak Pahari, sometimes described as a Panjabi dialect which, some 50–60 years ago, still had a written form (literature from this period, and before, is available in Kashmir). Some families speak Panjabi at home, and many use Urdu, the official language of Pakistan. Although none of the school's pupils speak Urdu as their mother tongue, or as their first language, all the families see Urdu as an important tie with Pakistan. The families are mostly of the Muslim religion, the mosque is close by, and almost all the children attend Urdu and Qur'anic classes in the afternoons and at the weekends. Urdu and Arabic (the language of the Qur'an) scripts are very similar, and it is possible to read this script in either language. Some families have visited 'home', as Kashmir is always referred to, often for months at a time, but the majority will not be returning there permanently, because of the war in the area. Their future is here.

Beginning reading

On a very ordinary school day I am reading and talking about books with my class. The children come to me individually, and together we read various books and stories. The term for this kind of reading activity, often and commonly used by practising teachers, is 'hearing children read'. Thus, from the onset, the young, and also the not-yet-reading children are both perceived and positioned as readers and active participators within this kind of early years practice. All this takes place well before they have learnt to read. The way this activity is, therefore, often referred to and presented to the children, is that the child 'reads' and the teacher 'listens'. Not only is this misleading because, as every teacher knows, what actually happens in these reading lessons is something far more complex and intriguing, but it may also provide a confusing starting point for children who do not yet perceive themselves as readers. Equally, too, parents may talk about *learning* to read first, with the emphasis on learning, rather than on reading. But as well as lacking a proper label, or name, perhaps more importantly, these lessons are not always explained, or structured in a way that would help the children to see their purpose, or to understand what is expected of them. Within these lessons, however, teacher and child interact endlessly: the child listens, tries to find out, asks and answers questions, remembers, memorises, takes risks, gives up, tries again – whilst the teacher reads, repeats, corrects, explains, asks and answers questions, smiles, frowns. In short, these lessons involve, in Vygotsky's (1986) terms, an entry into culture which is achieved by a transaction between the more skilled members who pass on, support, and instruct, and the less skilled ones, who through a process of internalisation, achieve new forms of consciousness and control.

For many emergent bilinguals who are learning to read in a new language and in a new cultural setting, some of the above dilemmas become immediately more problematic. The aim is to teach children to read, but as beginning reading is generally story based in Britain – while much of the language teaching, later on, is literature based – children will need particular cultural and linguistic knowledge from the earliest stages. First of all, this story-based approach may be very different to reading practices in other parts of the world (*see* Gregory 1993, for a contrast between English and Chinese practices). But furthermore, when children first start school, it is often assumed that by immersing the children in the reading practices of the school they automatically become acculturated into school literacy. Within our shared, collaborative early years reading practice, the teacher is the model and the child is the apprentice. The children are shown how a reader behaves, and they are expected to engage with the meaning of the story and respond to it personally: in essence the reader brings his/her own meaning to the text. But this becomes very complicated in any classroom, where the children's experiences are varied. Readers behave very differently in different cultural contexts, and all good stories have layers of meaning. But the layers of meaning do not refer to the text as much as to the individual acts of reading. This was poignantly revealed by Shirley Brice-Heath (1983) in her influential study of different reading practices in adjacent communities in South Carolina, which she observed and recorded in astonishing detail. Print carries values, and so do different readings, and these are always rooted in wider ideological beliefs and structures. English stories and English literature have a very specific place in the reading development in the British educational system. This is so firmly grounded in our practice and our theoretical understanding of reading development, that we often fail to see it as one cultural practice amongst many, and accept it as the norm.

The young reader

On this particular day, five-year-old Imrul (of Kashmiri/Pakistani background) is looking at the book he has chosen. It is *The Frog And The Fly* (Wood, 1985) and part of a very popular reading scheme used in British schools. The book tells a fairly simple story with large colourful pictures and with simple, minimal text. In the story a frog sits on a lily pad and captures a fly with its long, curly tongue. Imrul sits very close to me and rests his hand on my arm.

Teacher:	Let's have a look at the pictures. What can you see?
Imrul:	[No answer.]
Teacher:	[Whispering] What can you see?
Imrul:	Frog.
Teacher:	A frog... Ok...
Imrul:	Fly.
Teacher:	Yes, it is a fly, yes. This one?
Imrul:	Frog.
Teacher:	A frog, yes. There is a fly and a frog and this says... [pointing to the text and reading] A fly. A frog. What happens next? In this picture?
Imrul:	Fly away.
Teacher:	Yes. Where does the fly go?
Imrul:	To the water.
Teacher:	Sorry?
Imrul:	To the water.
Teacher:	To the water, and then?
Imrul:	A boat [pointing to a lily leaf].
Teacher:	Yes, it looks like a boat, perhaps. Is that a boat? [Pointing to another lily leaf.]
Imrul:	No.

Teacher:	What is it?
Imrul:	[No answer.]
Teacher:	A leaf.

And so we go on trying our very best to make sense of the story and each other. It soon becomes apparent that in order to read and understand this story much more is required than just knowledge of the language the story is written in which, on its own, of course, is not to be underestimated. But if reading, and understanding this story, is something more – indeed, if reading itself is more than the sum of the skills needed – how can this 'more' be defined, what does it mean for Imrul, and what implications does it have for me as his class teacher?

Learning to read English stories

I aim to unravel some of these questions, and during the following year I investigate the reading development of the young emergent bilingual children in my class in general and that of Imrul in particular. My observations begin to challenge the way I have been presenting reading to my pupils but, on this day, and throughout this reading lesson with *The Frog And The Fly*, I am still puzzling over Imrul's responses, which are all short answers to my direct questions. All his utterances reveal his own thinking, his ideas are logical and reasonable: a fly might disappear into water, and a lily pad could easily be a boat. But on the whole, he does not appear to understand the story. Each response makes sense but, put together, they do not seem to make a cohesive narrative in his mind. Clearly he is not yet reading with understanding, but neither is he sharing stories nor responding to stories with meaning or what is perceived as meaning. James Heap (1991) has raised the question of what 'counts' as reading, which leads me to wonder, what exactly counts as responding to stories with meaning? The programme of study for English in the Key Stages 1 and 2[1] of the National Curriculum (1995) presents contextual understanding as:

> ...focusing on meaning derived from the text as a whole. In order to confirm the sense of what they read, pupils should be taught to use their knowledge of book conventions, story structure, patterns of language and presentational devices, and their background knowledge and understanding of the content of a book. (DFE, 1995:7)

1   The subjects in Key Stages 1 and 2 are studied by children aged 5–11.

The deficit explanations which linger on within our schools – 'it is because these children do not have books at home and no one reads to them' – seem both inappropriate as well as inadequate. In fact, I am aware that many bilingual children in my class regularly spend afternoons learning to read at their community-language schools. But furthermore, the National Curriculum statement, cited above, is based on an assumption that contextual knowledge and understanding (about book conventions, story structures, patterns of language and so on) which, paradoxically, are highly culture specific, have already been acquired, somehow naturally, well before the child learns to read in English. Imrul and I carry on reading together:

Teacher:	What happens now, you tell me?
Imrul:	Spit water.
Teacher:	Oh, you think the frog, he spits out water on the fly. Mmmm, could be! Although, it's a different colour. It's pink, isn't it? Is it pink water?
Imrul:	[No answer.]
Teacher:	I think it's the tongue. Look at my tongue.
Imrul:	They got big tongue!
Teacher:	They've got massive, long tongues, yes!

Imrul enjoys each separate part or picture, but he does not seem to grasp the connection between the different parts. This puzzles me. It seems to me that he is not alone in this either as it happens to some other bilingual children in my class and, quite possibly, to some monolingual children in other classes and schools. There are various other occasions, too, when Imrul simply states – labels really – some of the things he can see in pictures, and though he is beginning to understand how English stories work and what lies behind the text in a reasonable and logical way, his guesses are often wrong. The level descriptors for reading at Level 1 in the English National Curriculum expect children to 'express their response to poems, stories and non-fiction by identifying aspects they like' (ibid. p. 19). Even though Imrul can do this, there is a notion, implicit in the assessment, that the child has to understand the story as a narrative. Purely identifying favourite aspects, perhaps unconnected and misunderstood, is not a response to a story which one would expect from a monolingual English child and, as Imrul is entitled to the same full curriculum as other children, he is also entitled to learn to respond to stories in the expected and accepted English way.

However, I fear that this lack of understanding may have an effect on Imrul's future motivation to share, to talk about stories, and ultimately on his progress in learning to read. Understanding the story, is often – and there is plenty of evidence to support this (Smith, 1985 and Meek, 1988) – cited as a motivating force for a young child to turn the page, to find out what happens next, which in return will enable the child to predict the next word, and to learn different ways of finding out what the actual words say. Furthermore, stories have a way of structuring experience. Carol Fox (1993) presents stories in the Chomskyan tradition, along with sentences as a universal structuring device, as stories and storying are such a universal phenomenon. Imrul, on the other hand, clearly knows about storytelling, because he regularly plays out stories with his models and his cars, but there seems to be a gap, that puzzles me, between his imaginative play and his engagement with written stories.

On another day, I watch Imrul as he picks up an Urdu book. He cannot read it as yet, and is simply looking at the text and the pictures. As I observe him I begin to see some of the traditions and experiences that are foreign to me but, that for Imrul, constitute real reading. I ask him about the book and listen to him as he begins to tell me about reading in Urdu. He knows about reading in the mosque, he knows about the Qur'an, and soon he begins to tell about Pakistan and Kashmir. Kashmir is a place where he has never been, but where he knows his family belongs and, as I listen to him, I am suddenly reminded of Karelia. Kashmir and Karelia – two very different, faraway places that stand worlds apart but are both, in essence, places that have been lost to the families who belong there. There are differences of course, but the emotions are surprisingly similar. The written fairy tales of my childhood, and the oral stories of my grandparents, all shaped my identity as they structured my experience and provided me with new words and new ways of expression. The stories I learnt then, in my childhood, the way they were told and what they told, have all shaped my understanding. I carry my previous reading experiences, the history of myself as a reader, with me; the same applies to Imrul and this Urdu book now, and will apply to him as he begins to read more widely in English and in Urdu and at his mosque classes.

This opens up a fresh new perspective for thinking about my bilingual pupils' reading, and the way they respond to English stories. It is liberating to begin to acknowledge the diversity of response as the norm, not an exception, or an oddity, and to accept the myriad web of values, traditions and histories that shape all children's understanding of reading, and which have an impact on the ways they engage with English stories. This must also have serious implications for my teaching of reading. I read some of Eve Gregory's (1994:119) work at this point in which she presents successful approaches developed in other parts of the world, approaches which attempt to respond to similar differences:

'difference' is used as a springboard for negotiation i.e. deliberate task-based strategies are designed which highlight and build upon difference; 'appropriate' knowledge needed for participation is made explicit, often through deliberate 'stage-setting' whereby children are asked to bear certain vital points in mind as they read a text or through 'modelling' of an appropriate style by the teacher; home/school learning programmes are based upon what caregivers are familiar with and understand rather than what the school feels they should understand.

As Imrul thinks about reading, it may evoke very different thoughts, feelings, ideas and experiences to mine. First and foremost, the role of religion in reading is crucially important to him and to his community, and very different to my own experience. But as I listen to Imrul and attempt to contrast his experiences with my own reading history, I suddenly remember the underlying notion of 'love thy God and thy Land', the intrinsic aim of my childhood's stories and the bedrock of the Finnish fairy tales. It is a pleasing discovery, and one that unites Imrul and me. But what exactly is 'appropriate knowledge' which will help me to teach Imrul to tune into reading in my class? The starting points are different, and so are the cultural practices, and it is difficult for both the teachers and learners to know where the similarities end and differences start. I begin by making arrangements to find out more about Imrul and his other reading practices, and in particular I want to find out what kinds of story – reading experiences Imrul will encounter at his community language classes.

Reading at the community language schools

The community language schools, together with the places of worship, are vitally important, often the lifeline of a minority community. It is these places and events, constructed around the religion or the language of the community, which generally pull and keep the people together, and so succeed in keeping the community and its culture and language alive. Imrul attends two community language classes, Urdu and Qur'anic, both of which have a very specific focus of learning to read. Urdu classes provide him an additional opportunity to develop, extend and consolidate Urdu vocabulary which will strengthen his linguistic and cultural ties with Pakistan, whereas the Qur'anic classes, in which he is learning to read in classical Arabic, a language he cannot speak, will teach him about his religion and provide him collective experiences of belonging to a Muslim community.

The hall, where the local Qur'anic class takes place, is big, bare and dark. The tables and chairs are neatly stacked against the walls. The wooden floor boards have recently been varnished, and there is a peculiar lingering smell. The teacher, always referred to as 'Auntie' by the children, is already there, and so are some of the children. They have pulled out some tables and chairs, and have started reading. More children, 24 in all and aged between five and 14 years, arrive, talking, laughing, pinching their noses, and holding their plastic carrier bags close to their body. They all know each other well. When I look at the outside of their plastic bags, I am still on the familiar ground and I can read the familiar high street names: Tesco, Sainsbury, Boots. But as soon as the children pull out their Qur'anic reading books, their prayer books or their beautifully gold-embossed Qur'ans, all the familiarity disappears, and I am immediately surrounded by a totally different kind of culture and reading tradition. An older boy is chanting his Qur'an; others recite on their own. They point to the text, as instructed, with their right index finger – and fiddle, of their own accord, with their carrier bags – and their voices soon become mixed up with the rustling of the bags. The strangeness of it all is an interesting experience.

Two older girls (aged 10 and 14) sit next to me and explain how they learnt to read the Qur'an. The girls' description of learning to read is similar to the approach I observed at a local Urdu class and, equally, it is easy to see some fundamental differences with my own school. At these community-language classes the children learn to recognise the whole of the alphabet first and learn to read short combinations of letters. At the Qur'anic classes this becomes progressively more difficult, whereas at the Urdu classes the children move from learning to read small words labelling pictures to slightly longer descriptions and short sentences still linked with pictures. At the Urdu classes the teachers had some story books from Pakistan, too, ready for the older, more fluent readers, but there were none for Imrul's age group. These Urdu books had several separate stories, often one on each page, and their pictures seemed to be illustrations of characters. Each story was a fable, or a myth, with an appropriate beginning (sort of 'once upon a time') that set the scene, and each story also had a distinct moral ending. These stories and, in particular, the moral endings, were considered very important for the children's overall development, for their general learning. But before Imrul was considered ready to read them, he had to become a fluent reader. Similarly here, at these Qur'an classes children never read stories, or engage in stories read to them. Yet, religious stories are vitally important, and will be told orally again and again, in Pahari at home, to the children to enable them to understand and learn religion, but at these classes the children concentrate on practising their reading.

Auntie interrupts us and, firmly but kindly, reminds the girls that they must close the Qur'an when they are talking: one should not talk over an open Qur'an. The girls resume their reading, and I think back to Imrul, my class, and my teaching of reading. I always begin to teach reading by talking around an open book. I encourage everyone to join in by discussing the story and the pictures. I ask questions and wait for answers. I expect children to express their own opinions and ask their questions. There are no concrete, tangible, reoccurring reading rituals like there are here. Washing yourself before the class, covering your head, holding your Qur'an and pointing to the text in a particular way, not talking when you are supposed to be reading, and the gender differences (boys chanting and girls reciting), all emphasise respect for reading the Qur'an and ultimately for Allah. Interestingly, at my school, the individual reading lessons do not have a proper name, a label; teachers simply talk about 'hearing readers'.

After a while the girls start testing each other to see if they can recite the difficult parts by heart. This surprises me, and I listen even more attentively. At one point the girls disagree on one word or sound. Auntie hears this and gives the girls the correct answer. 'What does it mean?' I find myself whispering. 'We don't know. We don't understand it. It's Arabic,' the girls answer. I look around again, and listen. I had known this all along, but somehow, had forgotten it, or had not quite accepted the relevance of it all. Somewhere at the back of my mind – though I was only aware of it later on – I had simplified this kind of reading. I had simplified the nature of the task, the range of words, sounds and nuances of sound, to a meaningless mumble. And the fact that the girls were keen to test each other, that they took a firm point of view when they disagreed, surprised me, but revealed the depth of their engagement in their reading. And yet, within the current English reading pedagogy, this kind of reading, memorising, reciting, learning by heart, is not perceived as real reading (see Wagner's 1993 account of Moroccan educational practices in which rote memorisation and learning extends to higher education). In our culture, and therefore, in our pedagogical reading hierarchy, individual reading for meaning is valued highly, and hence rated higher than reciting collectively for religious purposes.

Conclusion

So, for many emergent bilingual children in my class learning to read involves learning to read in three different languages (Urdu, Arabic and English) and at home the children speak a fourth one, Pahari. In each reading community the children meet its own set of people, whose roles in those sets vary. Each community uses different resources and different approaches to achieve its aims. The aims are diverse, and so are the values attached to these aims. Each reading community also has a history of its own, and the reading practices derive their meanings from this history and from the different historical and cultural traditions. Learning to read in English involves the very culture-specific ways of learning to engage with English stories, which as a process is perhaps more complicated than I had previously assumed. Marilyn Cochran-Smith's (1984) detailed and systematic observations of early literacy prompted her to question what is officially taught, what exactly the children need to learn, and how much of literacy is jointly undertaken through social interaction.

Much of our current reading pedagogy is based on an autonomous model of literacy which assumes a single model of literacy (Street, 1993), and because of this pedagogy – of which the phrase 'hearing children read' is so indicative – it is easy to be lulled into thinking that the early picture/story books are somehow relatively easy to interpret, and that children move smoothly, naturally, from story books to books with simple text and to story books with more text. This is conducive to overlooking the range of learning that has to happen before children, like Imrul, can be assessed in the school context as 'reading with meaning'. I had certainly assumed that all this story knowledge is learnt, and must be learnt, *before* children learn to read, not alongside at the same time, and especially not *after* they have learnt to read. But interestingly, Imrul's progression in learning to read proved the opposite. As the year goes by Imrul learns to read: first he learns to read names, then simple labels and words, then he learns to decode words by using a combination of letter names and phonics, and only later on, does he learn to read pictures and stories and to understand how English story books work. Reading and understanding stories are two separate areas which I need to teach.

Thus, the process of learning to read in my class includes learning the language of the text, learning to position yourself as a reader and an active participator within the school's reading events, learning to read the specific pictures and text, and crucially learning to understand (and perhaps accept?) some of the values attached to the school reading. In short, the children need to learn to belong to the school 'reading club', as Frank Smith (1985) explained, but as there are various different reading clubs or communities, in which bilingual children need to learn to belong, the whole process of joining in may be a highly complicated social and cultural issue. Needless to say, these were also issues I had not explicitly taught before but rather assumed that all the relevant and required knowledge and understanding is acquired swiftly, smoothly and almost naturally. The more specific customs, traditions and places of Kashmir are still relatively unknown to me, but I now know their importance to Imrul. I only need to think back to Karelia to remind myself how important these issues are to a five year old. As the year goes by, I begin to develop ways of modelling reading and understanding stories, ways of devising deliberate task-based strategies, and of making appropriate knowledge explicit. Some of this English reading knowledge and understanding can be achieved by discussing reading with Imrul, and with all the other children in my class. The children's interaction around the text and stories reveals the kinds of concerns and questions they have, but even more importantly, discussions can grow, as Paolo Freire (1972) wrote, into a critical and liberating dialogue between the teacher and the minority ethnic pupil. The journey from Karelia to Kashmir seems now much shorter than before.

References

Brice-Heath, S. (1983) *Ways with Words*. Cambridge: Cambridge University Press.

Cochran-Smith, M. (1984) *The Making of the Reader.* Norwood, NJ: Ablex Publishing Corp.

DFE (1995) *Key Stages 1 and 2 of the National Curriculum.* London: HMSO.

Fox, C. (1993) *At the Very Edge of the Forest: The influence of literature on storytelling by children.* London: Cassell.

Freire, Paolo (1972) *The Pedagogy of the Oppressed.* London: Sheed & Ward.

Gregory, E. (1993) 'Sweet and Sour: Learning to read in a British and in a Chinese School', *English in Education,* Autumn 1993, **27** (3).

Gregory, E. (1994) 'Cultural Assumptions and Early Years Pedagogy: The effect of home culture on minority children's interpretation of reading in school', *Language, Culture and Curriculum,* **7** (2), 111–24

Heap, J. (1991) 'A Situated Perspective on what Counts as Reading', in Baker, C. D. and Luke, A. (Eds) *Towards a Critical Sociology of Reading Pedagogy: Papers of the XII World Congress on Reading.* Amsterdam: John Benjamins Publishing Company.

Meek, M. (1988) *How Texts Teach what Readers Learn.* Stroud: The Thimble Press.

Smith, F. (1985) *Reading.* Cambridge: Cambridge University Press.

Street, B. (1993) *Cross-Cultural Approaches to Literacy.* Cambridge: Cambridge University Press.

Vygotsky, L. (1986) *Thought and Language.* Cambridge, Mass: The MIT Press.

Wagner, D. A., (1993) *Literacy, Culture and Development: Becoming literate in Morocco.* Cambridge: Cambridge University Press.

Wood, L. (1985) *The Frog And The Fly.* Oxford: Oxford University Press.

Author index

The bibliographical references at the end of each chapter are italicised. Where the same text is referred to in more than one chapter, only the first reference is given, e.g. Heath, S.B. Two italic references for the same author indicate two different texts.

Subject index